MW00603588

HUGO STINNES

By

HERMANN BRINCKMEYER

TRANSLATED FROM THE GERMAN BY
ALFRED B. KUTTNER

NEW YORK
B. W. HUEBSCH, Inc.
MCMXXI

CONTENTS

INTRODUCTION

There is a vast difference of opinion in Germany about Hugo Stinnes, but his name is on everybody's lips and his activities are the subject of constant discussion.

For many people he is an idol, for others he is a terror abroad in the land. The socialists of the *Vorwärts* look upon him as a necessary product of evolution and a pathfinder for the state of the future. According to Marxian theory, he is converting capitalism into the cocoon stage from which the finished butterfly of socialistic collectivism will some day emerge. He should therefore not be disturbed in his activities! Socialists may yet come to appreciate him

as one of their greatest figures. Socialists
of a different persuasion regard him as a
loathsome vampire of the proletariat. W.
von Moellendörf suspects Stinnes of being an
opportunist emancipated from all moral
considerations, whereas Walter Rathenau
characterizes him as a particularistic industrial baron whose work is destroying the
present system as a step towards collectivism. Sentimental Rhinelanders speak of
"Hugo" with the same respectful famili-
arity with which the Israelites may have
used the name of their leader in the desert.
And undoubtedly many a simple soul pic-
tures this enigmatic man as a just and stern
patriarch.

Stinnes is certainly no fine phrase-maker
or dreamer. He is never idle. While thousands of brain and manual workers are
standing by in despair, and thousands of
the most intelligent leaders are endlessly
discussing what kind of cement should be
used in the reconstruction of Germany,
this man, calm and unconcerned, is building

what may be either an edifice of steel destined to outlast time, or a Babylonian Tower that will plunge the builders into confusion.

HUGO STINNES

CHAPTER I

THE PERSONALITY OF HUGO STINNES

Hugo Stinnes has reached the age of fifty.
He has the appearance of a worker and
could go about in the clothes of a foreman
or a miner without attracting attention.
He is like a piece of coal wandering about
among his own coal mines.

His thick head is set upon a stocky trunk.
His black hair is cut close, the face is pale
and expansive, the beard is black as coal,
the nose is curved and the eyes are heavily
underlined. A German paper recently
called him the "Assyrian King."

His external appearance is devoid of pose,
he seems heavy and solid. He walks with a

slight stoop and shuffles along like a sailor. Clothes, habits and bearing denote a man of simple tastes. "His pale face, his rather tired eyes and his modest clothes make him look more like a labor secretary than a German Rockefeller"—to quote a French reporter who saw him in Spa.

Stinnes never stops working. It would certainly be a mistake to assume that he is driven by personal ambition, or money greed, or considerations of public welfare. Anyone who knows the captains of industry of the Rhine-Westphalian district in their own bailiwick, will understand him. These men have an irresistible impulse to do creative work. They are the engineers who organize human activity for constructive work; they know their building material through and through, and often go on scheming and figuring in their sleep, while dreaming about new combinations. These dyed-in-the-wool industrial leaders know nothing of rest, luxury, or enjoyment. They live and toil in the simplest surroundings. Even in their rare moments of leisure they have a preoccupied air, as if their minds were busy with problems. One cannot imagine men like Thyssen, Klöckner, Kirdorf or Stinnes at a cabaret. Nor will you find them in the false heroic pose of the period of Kaiser Wilhelm's romanticism. It is interesting to know that these men can drive through the workingmen's quarters in their automobiles without causing resentment. The laboring classes have an infallible instinct for workers and drones. Even the most radical class antagonist realizes that there is something more in men like Stinnes than the impulse to exploit, and the desire for luxury. Otherwise it would be inexplicable that even during the most agitated periods of revolutionary disturbance in the industrial section, no weapon has ever been raised against them.

These men are noted for their practical point of view. This is the source of their strength. Their nerves are fresh and are not influenced by emotions. But this exclusive devotion to practical considerations is also a source of weakness. These men lead a life of strict routine, and are chained to their work like convicts; they are out of the ordinary run and therefore they stand apart; they are the victims of their destiny. Many pages of the book of life are closed to them, though they are the rulers of life. No power of will can carry them beyond the walls which their own labors have built around them. They have no leisure and do not become patrons of the arts. Nor do they aspire to the fame of a Mæcenas.

For what do these men toil? By this time Hugo Stinnes has made a large fortune which is increasing from day to day; his power and his influence are incalculable. Even if he could take the time for it, he would find it impossible to spend all his wealth and enjoy it. But these men do not even take the time for rest which every other laborer claims. Thyssen, an old man of almost eighty years, rides to his office every morning at eight o'clock, in a street car, shoulder to shoulder with his own workmen. It is quite possible that these men never stop to think why they work.

Not long ago a foreman rode home with Stinnes at the end of a strenuous day. In the course of the conversation he asked him: "Tell me, Mr. Stinnes, why do you still work so hard?" Stinnes gave him a peculiar look and said: "For my children." Surely a curious answer! Did Stinnes mean it ironically, as a challenge to this inquisitive union man? Or was he unconsciously expressing the dynastic feeling of a family that has now been in the saddle for three generations? We know the importance which Hugo Stinnes attributes to the family, and especially to a family such as his. The unusual demands which he makes upon his relatives show that he expects them to live up to the family tradition.

The present activities of Hugo Stinnes

can hardly be surveyed. His associates are numerous and include men of great energy, experience, and efficiency. Some of them have had life-long experience in the management of great organizations, but Stinnes always remains in control.[1] It is noteworthy that his oldest son, Hugo, who may prove to be a greater business genius than his father, is developing an unusually independent initiative.

The personal fortune of Hugo Stinnes has been the subject of many conjectures, some of which are quite exaggerated. But we must not forget that the organizations which belong to him personally are relatively few in number compared to the numerous stock companies, participation companies, and family companies, which are included in the Stinnes Trust.

Hugo Stinnes has a genius for being detached and practical. Not only does he control his own organization with the

[1] *The Red Flag*, a socialist paper, recently published a poem which represents Stinnes in complete control of German industry, German business talent, and German politics.

highest mathematical intelligence, but he also has a sure instinct for practical combinations in every sphere of business. He recognizes economic possibilities with far-reaching implications while others still ignore them. He does not go in for over-ingenious schemes; he is always constructive. He can reverse his position at any moment without running the risk of disorganizing his work. These characteristics alone, however, would not be sufficient to make him a power in the Germany of to-day. There is the added factor that, in times when others lack will-power, his determination is firm; that in the midst of general instability, he has managed to remain unshaken. His poise and confidence are a part of his character and do not have to be paraded in public.

This is the secret of his power of suggestion over everybody with whom he comes in contact. Hence also the secret of his control of men and circumstances. His attitude towards labor and labor leaders is

2   7

peculiar to himself. His relations with the unions are conducted in a brusque tone. He does not take offense at unvarnished truths or even at downright rudeness, if it is honestly meant. As soon as he perceives that his opponent has a clear and succinct point of view, he is open to argument. He openly attacks mere tactics or else ignores them altogether. He is not friendly to theories. Occasionally he does not mind listening for an hour or so to a theorist. He likes to analyze and refute unsound theories, in the very act of listening to them.

He thinks in economic terms. When he proposes to have his employees participate in an enterprise by taking shares in it, he is guided by the thought of enlisting hitherto unutilized energies. In his socialistic projects, his idea is to have business benefit from the participation and joint responsibility of labor. Nevertheless he is a business aristocrat. This may be due to the fact that he does not feel that the period of collectivism has arrived, and because he knows that formal democracy breaks down in actual human relations, or perhaps he cannot help himself. As long as there is a general belief that reforms can be brought about by the mere fiat of theorists, he will probably continue to subject every new theory to the acid test of practical application.

During the recent debate in Germany about socializing all industries, Stinnes was frequently consulted. His position was that he did not reject collectivism but objected to having it established by decree. He did not dispute the theory but openly stated his conviction: "As regards the form of collectivism, you will always have to adapt yourselves to previous experience. Under no circumstances must you underestimate the importance of the individual." He always proceeds from the simplest experience: "When I am about to start a new enterprise I always ask two preliminary questions. In the first place, where is the man to organize it? Secondly, where are the efficient workmen? If these two requisites are lacking, I keep my hands off. This way of looking at the problem will have to be observed in the future. You must leave to the organizer what is the organizer's business—leadership. And you must see to it that labor gets a fair reward and a good living out of the enterprise."

Up to the present, the debate about socializing industries has not been able to solve this problem in any other way. Legien, the deceased leader of the German socialist unions, who had been in favor of putting socialism into practice immediately, arrived at the same conclusion, and acknowledged that the interests of both employer and employee must be consulted. In a conversation with Stinnes he once expressed himself as follows: "It is a pity that we did not get to know each other years ago; in that case many things in the labor movement and in industry might have turned out differently."

Stinnes has a remarkable influence upon
public opinion, yet he seldom appears in
public. His recent purchase of a string of
newspapers, which will be discussed later
on, led many people to surmise that he was
looking for a means of expressing his point
of view. But his acquisition of plants
covering the whole scale of production,
from cellulose factories and paper mills, to
printing establishments and publishing
houses, would seem to indicate that he is
more concerned with a large economic consolidation.

On one occasion, namely at the Spa conference, Stinnes did make a public declaration. He attended the conference as an
expert, and read his opinion about the coal
situation from a manuscript, in a high weak
voice which was in curious contrast to his
robust appearance. When he referred to
certain individuals being "afflicted with the
incurable illness of victory," he was cau-
tioned by the chairman of the conference
to moderate his words. Stinnes merely

looked up briefly from his manuscript and replied: "I am not here for the sake of being polite." His speech, which attracted wide attention, expressed his conviction that the reparation problem was a problem of European economics which could be solved only through the full coöperation of both the victors and the vanquished. Stinnes was speaking in terms of strict economic necessity, and his words echoed harshly in the rarefied atmosphere of diplomacy, tactics, and psychological subtleties which pervaded Spa.

The men of the Stinnes family have always clearly foreseen the steps of industrial evolution. Their efforts have decisively influenced economic development. To attain a correct estimate of Hugo Stinnes and his significance—for he is a force to be reckoned with—it is necessary to trace the enterprises of his family as well as his own earlier projects. Those who bear the name of Stinnes have never been communicative and have developed no theories. For that reason it is much more interesting and important to observe what they have done than to listen to what they have had to say.

CHAPTER II

THE history of the Stinnes family reflects a century's development of the Rhine-Westphalian industrial section, and with it of German economic history. The German development from the eighteenth to the nineteenth century was marked by political dissension, cramped economic conditions, small scale production, and petty politics among the guilds. But it was not long before the waves of political and economic upheaval swept over the country from the west, while technical advances in science and manufacture were making their first appearance in obscure workshops and laboratories.

Despite the system of small states, the Rhine - Ruhr district was already an economic unity at the beginning of the nineteenth century. Coal, iron, and water transportation formed the basis of industrial development. Steel from the famous Berg district, woolen goods from the manufacturing centres, silks and linens from the industrial centres of the Rhine were known in every country. To this day the saws of Remscheid, the locks of Velbert, the rivets of Altena, and the steel-ware of Solingen, have a traditional reputation throughout the world.

The northwestern part of Germany was the logical place for the development of industrial leaders. Krupp, Thyssen, Kirdorf, Haniel, and Stinnes, all developed into captains of industry with the aid of coal and iron. Their opponents, the most important representatives of modern socialism, also grew up in this region. Karl Marx was born in Trèves, at the junction of the Saar and the Rhine, Frederick Engels hails from the thriving Wupper valley, Bebel's cradle stood in the suburbs of Cologne, and Lassalle, coming from the eastern part of Germany, reached the height of his career in the Rhine district.

In the year 1808, Mathias Stinnes, the son of a shipping man who had gone into the transportation business on the Ruhr, made himself independent in Mülheim. Hardly eighteen years old, precocious, daring and determined, he was a genuine offspring of the district, having grown up in the midst of the coal fields and within sight of the Rhine, the oldest highway of communication in Europe. At that time just as at present, the French, whose revolutionary passion had been skillfully deflected into ambitious dreams of expansion by Napoleon, occupied the left bank of the Rhine. French rule brought about important changes in the Rhine lands. Petty politics and shortsighted economic policies had obstructed the Rhine at innumerable places, until the river, including the highways running along its banks, was little more than a prolific source of revenue for the states that bordered upon it. From Bingen to Bonn a merchant had to cross the border eight times, and from Germersheim to Rotterdam one had to pay duty at no less than 32 stations. At that time the abolition of duties and border restrictions was already under way, but the period of the Continental blockade soon intervened. Export on any large scale was restricted and the importation of raw materials was heavily penalized. It was of little benefit to Mülheim on the Ruhr to receive the status of a city from the French, in 1808. The atmosphere was not cleared until 1815, when the Congress of Vienna decided to incorporate the city with Prussia.

Thus, Mathias Stinnes had no easy time of it when he formed his company. On the Ruhr, it is true, he was not handicapped so much by existing conditions as on the Rhine. He bought his first coal barge, together with a quantity of coal, in 1810 for the price of 1240 German dollars. During the next decade he bought additional coal mines on the Ruhr. Soon after, his barges were to be seen on the Rhine. In 1817 Mathias Stinnes was already opening the important shipping line from Cologne to Rotterdam, with a regular service of nine of his own ships. At the same time he began to construct his own equipment; he built his ships in his own yards. From then on the firm expanded rapidly. By 1820, Mathias Stinnes owned 66 coal barges on the Rhine and the Ruhr, which plied regularly upstream on the Rhine to Bonn and Coblenz, and downstream to the Dutch maritime ports.

This was bound to lead to an expansion of the field of activity. The barges which took the coal north and south from Mülheim were loaded with colonial goods in Holland, and with salt in Wesel, from the royal reservation; from the Ruhr district they brought ironware and textiles as well as coal, and were loaded at the upper Rhine for the down trip with wine, dry vegetables, grain, and ores. Mannheim, which to-day is the reloading station for American grain, was at that time the shipping port for German grain destined for America.

For a long time this shipping business had to contend with various obstacles. The right to launch ships on the Rhine, and the freight rights of the Rhine ports were still restricted, and the navigation guilds exercised various monopolies. The Rhine navigation acts, which were unified in 1831 at Mainz, finally established freedom of communication on the Rhine. Mathias Stinnes contributed to no small extent to this improvement by taking things into his own hands and by presenting clever petitions to the authorities. There were most amusing controversies between the astute and farsighted shipping bosses of Mülheim, the "subject" Stinnes, and the bureaucratic officials of some of the government posts. Nor did Mathias Stinnes hesitate to undertake the complicated journey to Berlin whenever his interests required it. He is said to have had the same gift for overawing government officials with which his grandson, Hugo Stinnes, is credited to-day.

By 1831 the navigation acts had cleared the Rhine for Mathias Stinnes. The output at the mines, as well as the whole business of the district, immediately experienced a substantial increase through the opening up of a dependable market for all products as far as the territory of the upper Rhine and the Main. Mathias Stinnes made close connections with Mainz, Frankfurt, Worms, Mannheim, Karlsruhe, and Strassburg. He even did not hesitate to send his ships from the Rhine to Stettin and Hamburg, by way of the open sea. His enterprising spirit proved especially helpful to Mülheim when, together with Hugo Haniel, he undertook the development and equipment of the port facilities. He also built the pontoon bridges at Coblenz and Düsseldorf.

But his main interests continued to centre in the Rhine. As late as the forties, ships on the river were worked by means of hand- and horse-power, while downstream they drifted with the current. Sails could rarely be used. Though an occasional steamer had plied the Rhine before Stinnes' time, he was the first to use a real tug, and thus initiated the important Rhine freight service. It is worth mentioning that at that time the Exchequer held a long and circumstantial debate about the pros and cons of a state towing monopoly. This plan was debated interminably, until nobody any longer believed that it could be carried out. In the meanwhile, Mathias Stinnes ordered his first steam tug from the shipyards of Ditchborne & Marie, in London. The first Stinnes steamer plied on the Rhine in 1843. The Stinnes fleet remains to-day the biggest and most important fleet on the Rhine.

It was soon found that the first tug was not powerful enough. A second tug, built in Holland and christened "Mathias Stinnes I," became the head of a fleet of powerful tugs.

HUGO STINNES

At first there was considerable opposition to the use of steam power on the Rhine, as shown by an incident which occurred in 1848, when the tug "Mathias Stinnes I" had just begun its Rhine service with a fleet of barges in tow. There had been great excitement among the peasants and teamsters of the middle Rhine, who usually took charge of the ships at Cologne to tow them to the mines. They felt keenly the decrease in their earnings on account of the use of the tugs, and one day they decided to take matters into their own hands. It was secretly whispered about that something extraordinary was about to take place on the Rhine at Neuwied. The peasants and teamsters from the village of Weissenturm opposite Neuwied had conspired to set up a number of mortars and small cannon along the waterfront at Neuwied. When the tug came along with its barges in tow, a loud bombardment took place that raised the echoes from the neighboring mountains. The whole Rhine was thickly covered with clouds of smoke.

The inhabitants of Weissenturm hoped that at such a reception the hated tug would at once cut loose from its haul, and turn about face, never daring to come up from Mülheim again. But the conspiracy must have come to the ears of the captain, for the pilot house had been closely barricaded with iron plates, and not a soul was to be seen on deck. The whole line of boats passed quietly by, despite the bombardment. The peasants and teamsters had to resign themselves to their fate. But for many months the ship continued to navigate with its pilot house barricaded as a protection against further occurrences of this sort.

Mathias Stinnes, soon known as "old Matt," after having been in business for thirty-five years, perished in a railroad bridge accident at Hochfeld.

Every ship in the Stinnes fleet bears the name of its founder in addition to the serial number, and is known to every child on the Rhine. The type of ship, the kinds and quantities of goods carried, have of course changed appreciably. Whereas at the beginning of the Stinnes line the old wooden barges were about 200 tons burden, the type of steel barge most in use to-day can carry a load of from 1500 to 1700 tons. The most powerful Stinnes tugs tow four barges with an aggregate load of 6,000 tons, equal to the capacity of about 400 freight cars, and make about a mile and a half an hour, upstream. The great role which navigation plays in the Rhine-Ruhr district is revealed by the fact that the volume of freight, passing through the port of Duisburg on the Ruhr before the war, amounted to far over 20,000,000 tons annually, which is several million more than the freight traffic of Hamburg.

The founder of the house of Mathias Stinnes built up three main branches of the business; namely, mining, the coal trade, and transportation. When he died, in the year 1845, he left a firm of such wide ramifications and many-sided connections that his successor might well experience difficulty in keeping the business together. Several successors attempted to do this but failed. His son Mathias, Jr., popularly called "Little Mathias," had all he could do to keep the great firm going. The older Mathias had left detailed instructions as to the future policy of the business, and the close bonds that united the numerous members of the family forestalled any tendency to a division of interests. Nevertheless it was found necessary in 1848 to convert the firm of Mathias Stinnes, Limited into a stock company, called the "Mathias Stinnes Trading Corporation of Mülheim on the Ruhr," in order to assure its continued existence. At that time the Rhine and Ruhr fleets together comprised 60 coal barges. The firm had warehouses in Coblenz, Mainz, Mannheim, and Emmerich. It mined coal on four of its own mines known respectively, as the Victoria-Mathias mine, the Friedrich-Ernestine mine, the Graf Beust mine, and the Carolus Magnus mine. In addition, it had majority stock control in 38 other mines.

The following years revealed the solid foundations of the old firm of Mathias Stinnes. Before long a large part of the shares of the Mathias Stinnes Trading Corporation of Mülheim on the Ruhr, was again in the hands of the family. In 1860 the members of the family dissolved the corporation and reëstablished the former firm of Mathias Stinnes, Limited. Mathias Stinnes had left seven heirs, consisting of four sons and three daughters. Mathias Stinnes, Jr., died in 1853, when Gustav Stinnes, the second son of Stinnes, Sr., took over the management of the firm until his death, 1878. Thereupon, Herman Hugo Stinnes, the third and youngest son of Mathias Stinnes, headed the firm until his death in 1887. His wife was Adeline Coupienne, and their second son is the present Hugo Stinnes, born February 22, 1870.

HUGO STINNES

At its hundredth anniversary Mathias Stinnes, Limited, owned 21 tugs and 85 barges, having, in 1906, acquired the trading and shipping corporation of H. A. Disch of Mainz. It had also acquired the mine called "Mathias Stinnes," formerly Carnap, which became the most important of all its mining properties.

The Stinnes family has played a very important part in the organization of the Ruhr coal industry. The members of the family are among the founders of three important combines in the Ruhr district. These are the Confederation of Mining Interests under the Jurisdiction of the Board of Mines for Dortmund, founded in 1858, which has been largely responsible for the technical development of mining; the Rhine - Westphalian Coal Syndicate, formed in 1893, which regulated the production, price, and distribution of the Ruhr coal deposits; and the Rhine Coal and Shipping Company, formed in 1903 and known as the "Coal Bureau." This so-called "Coal Bureau" and the Rhine-Westphalian Coal Syndicate, usually called the "Coal Syndicate," control the production and distribution of coal in the entire Ruhr district.

In the course of a century's growth, the firm of Mathias Stinnes, Limited thus branched out into transportation, commerce, and mining, on an imposing scale.

CHAPTER III

STINNES began his career under favorable conditions. Even in these days of free opportunity Germany can show no industrial leader of the calibre of a trust magnate who has reached the pinnacle of his power by climbing up from the bottom. Klöckner, Krupp, Rathenau, Siemens, are all men who have developed their inheritances. The German industrial field has been pretty well divided up. It is necessary for the individual to grow up in it, in order to achieve importance. Anybody coming from the outside is bound to find it difficult to take root in this soil. Otto Wolf is the exception which proves the rule. But his success lies almost exclusively in the field of commercial enterprise. Perhaps it is due to the gigantic concentrations of modern business which lead to the absorption of numerous independent concerns which cannot resist this process, that new men are more likely to reach a commanding position within this field. The Stinnes Trust shows numerous examples of this. Several directors of the Stinnes enterprises have risen from labor circles.

But it is not enough to be a son or a grandson to ensure success. Respected old names are constantly disappearing. Besides an inheritance and a tradition behind him, the industrial leader of to-day must also have a large measure of power, efficiency, and personality.

Hugo Stinnes had the tradition and the widely ramified connections of his family. The inheritance in itself did not amount to much. After a short period of commercial apprenticeship in Coblenz, he learnt the mining business both above and below ground at the Wiethe mine. At the age of nineteen he attended a school of mining.

Then he took a position in the firm of Mathias Stinnes, Limited. After two years he did not feel himself suited there, and at the age of twenty-three he formed his own firm under the name of Hugo Stinnes, Limited. He also continued as director of mining operations in the family mines. The paid-in capital of his firm amounted to 50,000 marks.

It is extraordinary how the characteristics and tendencies of the old Mathias Stinnes reappear in his grandchild. One finds the same restless spirit, the same daring, the same talent for combinations and constructive effort. But the field of activity for these powers is infinitely greater. Never before have the opportunities in German industry been so favorable to constructive business genius as they are to-day.

Up to a short time ago, the organizers of gigantic trusts on the American scale were unknown in German industrial life. For years there had been powerful combinations of finance and industry under various leaderships, and several large enterprises, such as those of Thyssen and Kirdorf, had enjoyed a period of astonishing growth, due to favorable opportunities and the daring of those in charge. But it sounded incredible to Germans before the war, that the industry of the United States should be dominated by five men. Carnegie's United States Steel Corporation and Rockefeller's Standard Oil Company, which deal in millions, were regarded by them as examples of industrial empires.

These magnates could not achieve their billion-dollar eminence without the aid of unlimited stock manipulation, unscrupulous methods in killing competition, and unbridled speculation. A dissolution of all established economic organizations, and the rapid development of absolutely new forms of organization have taken place in Germany since the war. The extent to which this has gone is best indicated by the fact that American methods of financing, of pooling of interests, and of combinations, have already been adopted in Germany, and are undergoing further development.

At the height of the trust period in America, the London *Economist* estimated that the five magnates, Rockefeller, Harriman, Morgan, Vanderbilt, and Gould, were worth over three billion dollars and controlled over thirty billion dollars, which represents the greater part of the total American capital invested in banks, railroads, and industries. This gave them a very considerable control of the industrial life of the United States.

A large consolidation movement of German industry got under way in the nineties. The freedom of trade in the nineteenth century had promoted a concentration of power in industry, commerce, and also in agriculture, which led to strong opposition from the smaller business interests, as well as to a fierce competitive struggle between those in control. But a small cycle of industrial crises sufficed to make even the most solid business men recognize on what insecure foundations their enterprises were based. Thus, various industrial groups entered into combinations. At first the emphasis was laid upon common interests. Coalitions of employers and employees were formed in every branch of industry in order to secure the most favorable conditions for both parties. These defensive organizations of various units in the industry were followed by consolidations into larger groups, which took the form of syndicates and cartels. Here certain limitations upon independent organizations were mutually accepted for the purpose of avoiding the slowing up of sales, price fluctations, and the effects of crises. At the same time, associations were formed for reducing the cost of production and retail prices.

These consolidations brought about a general weakening of the excluded industrial units and led to fusions, especially within the industry. This was but a step removed from concentration on a large scale in that, for example, a syndicated business on the basis of cheaper raw materials could be operated more profitably than other isolated concerns which the syndicated business absorbed one after the other.

The system of stock companies favored this development and in many cases was necessary to make it possible. It is generally admitted that in former days, before government regulation was introduced, American corporations were often none too scrupulous about the law. They introduced many new methods of stock participation and of pooling of interests, which frequently were by no means to the advantage of the general public. Some of these methods have come into general use and have also been adopted by German corporations. · It is no longer a secret that the combinations of transportation systems and other industrial interests can easily lead to a concealment of the actual assets of companies, and in fact frequently do so. They also lead to consolidations of so complicated a nature that they pass beyond the power of any individual to survey.

These companies may often be compared to the numerous links of a chain which are under the control and direction of anyone who has the first link in his hands. The system of preferred shares, with multiple voting power, increases the possibilities of exerting influence still more. At the same time the owners, despite their comparatively small capital investment, have the determining vote in all important decisions of the company. In this way it is easily possible, under certain circumstances, for a small group to dominate affairs at will without much outlay of capital. These methods are justified at present on account of the danger of foreign control, due to the exchange situation. But the fact remains that it is always possible for a small group to bring a greater and greater section of industry under its control.

Anyone who has the influence to put through a scheme of industrial control can do so nowadays on a much larger scale than ever before. And it is open to anyone to misuse this power. Unless Germany is willing to be exposed to contingencies and surprises of a most startling nature, she will soon have to recognize the necessity of investigating and controlling this highly complicated situation.

The movement towards consolidation is well under way in German industry. Hugo Stinnes is one of the main forces behind these developments. Mining, the coal business, and water transportation, form the fulcrum from which he operates, as was the case with his grandfather Mathias Stinnes. He runs his own mines and ore-concentration plants. He acquires ships for commerce both on inland waterways and on the high seas. He is a coal dealer with international markets. He has his branches on the continent and overseas. His ships are to be seen on rivers and canals, on the North Sea and the Baltic, on the Mediterranean, and on the Black Sea.

HUGO STINNES

Hugo Stinnes began to exert an influence upon the construction of the entire German industrial edifice very early in his career, through the organization and the various combinations of his companies. He is one of the controlling figures in the consolidation movement in the mining industry. The Rhine-Westphalian coal district, which a hundred years ago was run by patriarchal operating units on a small scale, in the course of the nineteenth century became the scene of large-scale capitalistic operations which frequently had recourse to unscrupulous methods. After the union of the Ruhr district with Prussia, the industrial forces were increased through the immigration of large bodies of laborers, and the appearance of more and more employers. Many of these employers were guilty of ruthless exploitation and short-sighted methods of administration, so that they were not unjustly accused of putting the slogan "Business is business," before every other consideration. Wild promotion and unbridled competition combined with panics to bring about uncertain times for the mining operations. Production and price agreements and control of distribution were evolved with increasing frequency from about 1870 on, as a defense against these tendencies.

We have already seen that the Stinnes family had always been a leader in such endeavors. It is therefore not astonishing to find young Stinnes familiar with this development. He soon played a leading role in the Rhine-Westphalian Coal Syndicate. The syndicate now includes practically the entire coal ouput of the Ruhr basin, and regulates production, prices, and consumption. In the same way Hugo Stinnes is a power in the Coal Bureau— the very name is indicative of the practical spirit of this district—which has been in existence since 1903, having brilliantly organized the market for Ruhr coal. The Rhine - Westphalian Coal Syndicate, the firms of Mathias Stinnes, Limited and

Hugo Stinnes, Limited, and a number of the other companies have considerable capital invested in the Coal Bureau.

Hugo Stinnes soon added the production of iron and steel to the production of coal. The German-Luxemburg Mining & Smelting Company became his main sphere of activity.

The district of German-Luxemburg was developed with uncanny rapidity. At the end of the nineties, the Differdingen Blast Furnace Company, Inc., in Luxemburg, and the Dannenbaum Mining Company were combined into the Differdingen-Dannenbaum Iron & Coal Company. But this company did not last and was soon liquidated with considerable loss to the stockholders and creditors. The German-Luxemburg Mining & Smelting Company, Inc., with a capital of 1,000,000 marks, was formed in 1901 at Bochum. This corporation took over the Differdingen - Dannenbaum Iron & Coal Company. Within the year the capital stock was raised to 25,000,-000 marks, and by 1910 this figure had been increased to 60,000,000 marks. The German-Luxemburg Mining & Smelting Company has an interest in the Saar-Mosel Mining Company and thus procures the coal for the Differdingen plant at a considerable freight saving.

Soon after this, the German-Luxemburg Mining & Smelting Company was further increased by the addition of the Union, a technically highly developed corporation engaged in the mining and iron and steel business at Dortmund. On this occasion the capital was again increased so that it now reached 100,000,000 marks. In this way the German-Luxemburg Mining & Smelting Company developed into the Differdingen Smelting Company, whose main business consisted in exporting to Frankfurt, Belgium, and countries oversea; it thus became a counterpart of the Rhine-Westphalian industrial district. Several mines were added as the basis for a coal supply for the Dortmund works. In order to utilize the Saar coal, the production of iron was increased through the addition of the blast furnaces and steel mills of Rümelingen and St. Ingbert.

Altogether the German-Luxemburg Mining & Smelting Company comprises establishments at Bochum, Dortmund, Mülheim on the Ruhr, Emden, and at Differdingen (Luxemburg), though the last has been taken away through the liquidation resulting from the treaty of peace. The greater part of the mining establishments is situated in the Ruhr basin. Here the company owns the coal and iron-ore works of Dannenbaum, the mines Prinz Regent and Friedlicher Nachbar, the factory at Hasenwinkel, and the series of mines of Bruchstrasse at Langendreer, Wiendahlsbank at Annen, Adolf von Hansemann at Mengede, Glückauf Tiefbau, Karl Friederich's Erbstolln at Stiepel, Kaiser Friedrich at Barop, Luise Tiefbau and Tremonia at Dortmund.

Besides this, the company is interested in the Rhine-Westphalian Mining Company at Mülheim (Ruhr). The total production of the coal mines amounts to over 5,000,000 tons annually. The coke produced annually amounts to 1,300,000 tons. The by-products consist of considerable quantities of ammonia, tar, benzol, and other products.

The plants at Dortmund, which have an exceptional technical equipment, include six blasting furnaces and one steel plant, besides rolling mills, pressed steel mills, and foundries. It also has its own plants to continue the manufacturing process up to the finished product. All kinds of materials and accessories for the construction of railroad engines and rolling stock are manufactured at Dortmund. The electric establishments are equipped with all the latest improvements in mining technology. The Dortmund works also include the Horst iron and steel works with their own blast furnaces, a screw factory, a wagon-spring factory and a series of subsidiary factories. The ore for the Dortmund Union is supplied primarily from its own iron-ore mines on the Ruhr, in the district of the Sieg

River, on the Weser River, in Nassau, and in the Harz.

The mining syndicate, Friedrich Wilhelm, at Mülheim-on-the-Ruhr, has belonged to the German-Luxemburg Mining & Smelting Company since 1905. This establishment owns a large number of its own mining fields, and up to the war had a share in the Lorraine mines. The mine at Mülheim includes five blast furnaces capable of producting 220,000 tons annually. Large foundry establishments manufacture machine parts, castings and pipes. A large number of establishments with the most up-to-date special machinery continue the process of manufacture of steel products. They specialize in mining and foundry machinery, so that the German-Luxemburg Mining & Smelting Company is in a position to supply its own technical equipment.

Since 1911 the German-Luxemburg Mining & Smelting Company has been linked up with the North Sea works at Emden. The factories there are being enlarged in conjunction with the recent Helling establishments. The North Sea factories are interested in the production of coal, in the coal trade, and in the sale of benzol, ammonia, and tar, through the agency of a number of companies.

The Hohenzollern foundry, situated at Emden, which belongs to the German-Luxemburg Mining & Smelting Company, has its own mine fields in Upper Frankonia and in the Upper Palatinate.

Through the North Sea works at Emden, the German-Luxemburg Mining & Smelting Company is interested in the German Navigation Company, "Midgard," at Bremen, in the Rhine Navigation Company, and in the Mannheim Towing Company, which provide it with sea and river transportation facilities.

Before the liquidation, brought about by the treaty of peace, extensive factories in Differdingen and Lorraine belonged to the German-Luxemburg Mining & Smelting Company. The Differdingen works owned ten blast furnaces in the immediate vicinity of the mines, as well as numerous other factories almost entirely engaged in manufacturing iron girders. Since 1911 these works had been connected with the mining and foundry establishments of Rümelingen and St. Ingbert through a joint agreement.

Hugo Stinnes organized and administered this gigantic enterprise with great success. By means of the saving in freight rates, and by perfecting the management, he made it possible to concentrate upon the production of a highly developed finished article, and at the same time to make the business extraordinarily profitable. The German-Luxemburg Mining & Smelting Company, with more than 40,000 employees, thus became one of the leading mining establishments, of the greatest importance both for the home market and for the export trade.

A second enterprise of gigantic proportions, the Rhine-Westphalian Electric Company, grew up under the direction of Hugo Stinnes while the German-Luxemburg Mining & Smelting Company was developing. This was founded in 1898, and first took over the management of an electrical plant in Essen-Ruhr. From the very beginning the object of this enterprise was extraordinarily far-reaching. The Company was intended to supply the whole Rhine-Westphalian industrial district with electric power. The power plant at Essen was erected in immediate connection with the old Stinnes mine of Victoria-Mathias. In the eastern part of the Ruhr coal basin a second modern plant was erected at the coal mine Wiendahlsbank, which belongs to the German-Luxemburg Mining & Smelting Company. By 1908 the Rhine-Westphalian Electric Company had already become so large that the eastern plant was combined with the Westphalian Electrical Works, Inc., under one joint management. The territory supplied by the Rhine-Westphalian electrical power stations extends from the Dutch border on the north to the Ahr valley in the south, and almost entirely includes the government districts of Düsseldorf and Cologne, with all their townships.

In addition, the Company developed the gas and water supply, and since 1912 has undertaken to supply the gas for 25 cities and townships. The directorship of this electrical industry is very interestingly organized. The ownership of the Rhine-Westphalian Electric Company is in the hands of both individuals and municipalities. The cities of Essen, Mülheim-on-the-Ruhr, Ruhrort, Solingen, Gelsenkirchen, and numerous other municipalities, own shares in the Company.

In the natural course of its development, the Rhine-Westphalian Electric Company undertook to supply the Rhine-Ruhr district with a comprehensive network of street-car systems and small gauge railroads.

Thus Hugo Stinnes is inextricably associated with the Rhine-Westphalian industrial district. By virtue of the many directorships which he holds, he is in close touch with every business of any importance in this industrial section.

Besides this, he has also devoted special attention to the German seaboard. He had already anticipated the close connection of his industrial district with ocean transportation, in founding a small establishment at Harburg-on-the-Elbe. This was followed by the formation of the firm of Hugo Stinnes Shipping Company, Limited, for the purpose of going into the shipping business on a large scale. This firm soon owned 13 of its own steamers with which it carried coal, ore, wood, and grain, to various European ports.

CHAPTER IV

HIS PART IN THE WORLD WAR

THE activities of Hugo Stinnes during the
period of the World War have given rise
to a great deal of contradictory discussion.
It will be a long time before we shall be
able to see what was going on behind the
scenes in Germany on the industrial side
of the war, and much of what happened
there may never be fully cleared up. It
is generally known that for many business
men, and especially for those engaged in
the major industries, the war turned out
to be a period of extraordinary industrial
acceleration. In a state which in normal
times shows little sympathy for collectivism,
it is of course to be expected that a period of
war will bring out the same clash of interests
that characterizes a highly individualized

industry, and will even sharpen these conflicts still more. We must also remember that though there was an accurate plan for general military service, not even the most primitive arrangements for general industrial service in war times had been prepared.

So indefatigable a business man as Hugo Stinnes could not be expected to remain idle in a period of universal activity. He necessarily made the greatest possible use of every opportunity, without reflecting particularly about the unfortunate causes that had made these opportunities possible.

The liquidation of industries in occupied Belgium forms a chapter of its own. The industrial war of the Entente, the blockade, and the influence exerted upon neutrals, called for counter-measures on the part of the Central Powers. The liquidation in Belgium was entrusted to the German industrial leaders. Three companies were formed in the Ruhr industrial district: the Industrial Company, Limited, the Transportation Company, Limited, and the Mining Company, Limited. All these companies were formed in 1916. Among those interested in these •companies were Friedrich Krupp, Inc., the Phönix Company, the Gute Hoffnung Smelters Company, and the German-Luxemburg Mining & Smelting Company, Inc. This last company included Hugo Stinnes. These three companies played a great part in carrying out the proposed measures for taking over the Belgian industries. They were especially favored in regard to the purchase and management of Belgian factories. They further secured for themselves the exclusive right of purchasing coal and metal mines, and factories, and ran the Belgian gas, water, and electric works. The further plans of these companies were, of course, cut short by the outcome of the war.

During the war, Hugo Stinnes greatly strengthened his grip upon German industry. He gave his special attention to the development of the trade and transportation possibilities at his command. The

Hamburg shipping trade formed a combination with the metal industries. At this time Albert Ballin made the following statement: "The Hamburg American Line intends to consolidate its interests more definitely and completely than hitherto, with the capitalistic groups of our key industries and our banking system."

Stinnes acquired an interest in various oversea steamship lines and mercantile firms. In 1918 he became interested in the Woermann Line and in the German East-African Line. He established close connections with the Hamburg American Line and the North German Lloyd Line. Before this, the Stinnes Trust had already taken over several importing firms, among them the coal business of H. W. Heidmann at Hamburg, together with its wharves and steamers. In the fall of 1917, Stinnes formed the Hugo Stinnes Ocean Navigation and Trading Company, Inc. His son is especially active in this company.

Since the middle of 1918, Stinnes has also

been interested in the German-American Petroleum Company of Hamburg. Stinnes bought the Hamburg City Hall Hotel, and the Hotel Hamburger Hof. These big buildings were converted into offices and were used to house the various Boards of Directors and their executive staffs.

Additional mercantile firms in Königsberg and Bremerhaven were added to Stinnes' shipping combine, together with the Baltic Navigation Company at Flensburg. Eleven large steamers were ordered from various German shipyards. After the war, the entire ocean transportation of the Stinnes Trust was to be handled by the Stinnes fleet.

At the same time Stinnes secured vast land holdings in East Germany with extensive forests, in the interests of his mining business. The forests were intended to provide the mining timber for the Stinnes mines. Towards the end of the war, the Stinnes Trust also acquired interests in the Rhine lignite deposits. Thus a mighty industrial unit, developed and directed with great forethought, had been brought together under the powerful leadership of Stinnes just before the revolution broke out.

CHAPTER V

THE MINING TRUST: THE RHINE-ELBE-UNION[1]

THE revolution in Germany after the war gravely threatened the complicated structure of German industrial life. Ballin, the director of the Hamburg American Line, saw his life work destroyed, and retired from the scene. During this period Hugo Stinnes' nerves remained unruffled. The peace treaty was signed, and important sections of the German industry were detached from the main body. The German-Luxemburg Mining & Smelting Company lost all its enterprises in the southwest, including its iron-ore and coal supply. In the last year before the war, the southwestern district had produced the enormous

---

[1] Rhine-Elbe is the name of a Gelsenkirchen mine, and Union stands for a Dortmund factory of the German-Luxemburg Mining & Smelting Company.

amount of 750,000 tons of pig iron for the German-Luxemburg Mining & Smelting Company, and had mined 1,000,000 tons of coal, amounting to 60% of the entire output of the Company. The Company tried to retain the Differdingen works, situated in Luxemburg, but the ore deposits upon which these factories depended were located in Lorraine. Thus this enterprise also had to be sacrificed. The connection with the plant at Rümelingen-St. Ingbert was likewise destroyed.

In this way the German-Luxemburg Mining & Smelting Company lost its entire investment in the southwest. A French group replaced the Stinnes Trust in Luxemburg and Lorraine. This was a vital blow to the Company, although the purchase price received from the French Company put considerable cash at its disposal. An important source of supply for running the factories could also be counted upon through an agreement, made for a period of thirty years, according to which a considerable proportion of the ore requirements of the German-Luxemburg Mining & Smelting Company was assured.

As a result of the loss of St. Ingbert, the German-Luxemburg Mining & Smelting Company had to cast about for new manufacturing plants in order to be able to supply the necessary intermediate products for the manufacture of the finished goods. As it was impossible to erect any new buildings, the Company acquired a number of old factories. Among these were the steel works of the Brüninghaus Company, Inc., and the firm of Friedrich Thomée, Inc., both situated at Werdohl, as well as the firm of Karl Berg, Inc., at Eveking. These factories were adopted for manufacturing bar and plate steel, as well as castings, springs, and wagon parts. Further purchases included the steel roller mills of Meggen, the chain factory of Karl Schliepers in the city of Grüne, and the rivet factory of Knipping Brothers at Altena.

But these protective extensions of the industry did not satisfy Stinnes. He developed a project capable of continuing the unprecedented growth of the German-Luxemburg Mining & Smelting Company, despite all its adversities. His attention had been directed to the Gelsenkirchen Mining Company, Inc., another gigantic mining business which had also been crippled and reduced through the treaty of peace.

The Gelsenkirchen Mining Company, Inc., was the work of the brothers Emil and Adolph Kirdorf. It was founded in the year 1873 as a mining business, employing a thousand men, and for a long time, confined itself to coal mining. Important consolidations gradually enabled the business to attain a commanding position in the district. In 1913 it employed 55,000 hands, and its share in the Rhine-Westphalian Coal Syndicate amounted to 10,000,000 tons, representing 11% of the whole Syndicate. The expansion of the Gelsenkirchen Mining Company, Inc. was at first in a horizontal direction, but after 1905 it undertook to expand vertically, through a consolidation of the coal-consuming industries with the coal producers, especially through consolidations with mining syndicates at Aix-la-Chapelle and at Schalk.

The terms "horizontal" and "vertical" as applied to trusts require a word of explanation. A horizontal trust approximates the familiar type of American trust which is usually a consolidation of all the units of a particular industry, engaged in the production or manufacture of a single kind or type of product. The object of such a trust is to produce an article as economically as possible and to exercise a monopolistic control over it. The Standard Oil Company is an excellent example of this kind of trust. A vertical trust is a complete and self-contained consolidation of all the successive stages of manufacture from the production of raw material to the final distribution of the finished article. It is an industrial cycle completely protected at both ends, with every source of supply and every stage of production in the same hands. If the Standard Oil Company acquired coal and iron mines to manufacture its own supply of oil machinery, tanks, and pipes, controlled its own railroads to handle its tank cars, and built its own tankers in its own shipyards, besides controlling the automobile industry in order to find a market for its gasoline, it would approximate the German idea of a vertical trust.

Besides its mines and ore fields, the Gelsenkirchen Mining Company, Inc., soon included blast furnaces, steel works, wire factories, and similar plants. This company laid great stress upon the extension of its ore basis. As the interest charges were unusually heavy, the Kirdorf brothers were compelled to pay especial attention to the reduction of production costs. They skillfully foresaw the necessity of technical improvements, and their enterprise became distinguished for its gigantic buildings and the modern methods constantly introduced.

Thus in 1913, the cost of new buildings and developments was estimated at 60,000,000 gold marks. The result of the war was a catastrophe for this concern. It was forced to pay terrible penalties for its expansion into the Minette district, another German mining field. It had to give up its diversified enterprises and return to mining. For this reason Stinnes could count upon a friendly reception from the Gelsenkirchen Mining Company when he undertook a rapprochement. It was a matter of sheer necessity for both Kirdorf and Stinnes to come together. Nevertheless Kirdorf, who has always been known for his independence, must have found it very painful to combine his life work with that of another man. The consolidation went into effect in July, 1920. The control of the two businesses rests with the Rhine-Elbe-Union. The leaders of this consolidation, besides Stinnes, are General Director Vögler of the German-Luxemburg Mining & Smelting Company, and Emil Kirdorf.

HUGO STINNES

The German-Luxemburg Mining & Smelting Company and the Gelsenkirchen Mining Company have entered into an agreement which is to hold good for eighty years. They now complement each other and mutually aid each other's development. They form a mining business based upon broad foundations, and are starting under the most favorable auspices. Their consolidation into the Rhine-Elbe-Union is to last until the year 2000.

CHAPTER VI

THE ELECTRO-MINING TRUST: THE SIEMENS-RHINE-ELBE-SCHUCKERT-UNION

THESE tendencies to form gigantic fusion and expansions in German industry cannot be entirely ascribed to personal ambition or to the craving for power. The driving forces are of an economic nature. Before the war, Germany had an annual increase of population which amounted to more than the entire population of a large city like Detroit or Buffalo. The amount of arable land did not keep pace with this increase. The number of emigrants was inconsiderable. For this reason, an increased productivity from year to year was necessary in order to keep up the standard of maintenance. Compared to any other country Germany had a very small number of people

64

not engaged in productive labor. Nevertheless, the production of goods from the country's own raw materials was insufficient to cover the basic needs. It was therefore essential to export on a considerable scale, either through the direct shipment of raw materials for foreign needs, or through manufacturing indigenous and imported raw materials into finished goods for export and re-export. In order to ensure adequate profit from this export trade, it became more and more necessary to protect the raw material, that is, to convert it at home into partly or entirely finished goods. For this purpose it was necessary to do the manufacturing at home, and to produce goods of the finest and most varied grades of workmanship. It was essential to make the raw material yield the greatest possible increment of profit and wages before the goods passed out of the country.

Under these conditions it was necessary to develop this so-called continuing industry, and to foster technical improvements as carefully as possible. Quite aside from the unavoidable export of raw materials, Germany therefore tended more and more to supply foreign markets with the greatest possible number of the finest grades of manufactured goods, chemicals, tools, articles of general use, dye-stuffs, medicines and similar goods. At the same time, it was necessary to increase the output and the profit of the industries as much as possible in order to compete in the markets of the world.

This development was bound to lead to consolidation, mergers and trusts. Factories producing the same or similar goods worked more economically and showed a greater yield by manufacturing according to a joint agreement and avoiding duplication. The consolidation of industry, and the process of building it up upon the natural foundation of raw materials increased the productivity, saved transportation goods, and met the special needs of finished-goods manufacture. German in-

66

dustry could not afford to have friction and opposition between its industrial enterprises. A certain amount of speculation was inevitable but this did not attain large proportions.

War and revolution have not improved the industrial situation of the German people. Losses in population, territory, and materials have been very great. Exports and imports have also been curtailed, and besides this, the heavy mortgages of the treaty of peace on which both interest and capital must be paid, weigh heavily upon German industry. Billions of paper marks and much theoretical discussion have not been of the slightest help in raising production. Germany must produce in order to live, and must produce more, better, and cheaper goods than before.

Thus the combination of industry has become inevitable. The elasticity with which alterations and consolidations are being carried out is astonishing. This is partly achieved by technical and industrial methods. The scarcity of coal, for instance, has led industries to adopt lignite to an extent previously considered impossible. Petroleum is beginning to be utilized to an astonishing degree. New methods of chemical production are being invented every day. The discovery and application of new methods promise very interesting results. The expensive experiments necessary for this development are being made in the field where a high degree of industrial combination has already taken place.

The introduction of better industrial management and new forms of economic organization is also helping to increase and improve production. But industrial management, plans for socializing industries, and industrial councils, are all schemes about which there is still very little agreement. In the meanwhile, the consolidation movement is making headway. There are very few isolated factories left. In some branches of industry, isolated enterprises have entirely disappeared. German national industry is gradually becoming a multicellular, but unified industrial body. The art of management is becoming an exact science, and the whole process of production is becoming an organized cycle under the direction of a single mind.

This development has made most progress among the consolidated industries, where the horizontal and vertical systems of industrial organization were first invented and applied. The horizontal system seeks to apply the most rational and highly specialized methods to some particular stage of the manufacturing process after it has been brought together under a unified management and carries the process of standardization to the furthest possible stage. Thus the competitive struggle between factories engaged in the same process is either lessened or altogether abolished, and the technical connection with the next stage of manufacture is made with much less waste and friction.

The vertical system seeks to unite the

whole manufacturing process under the same management, and to start the raw material on a cycle in which it is progressively manufactured until it emerges as the finished article. Every stage of the process must be controlled and coördinated with the succeeding stage. Thus for example, the process would run from coal and ore through pig iron, steel, casting, to tools, machines, and electro-technical equipment.

The Rhine-Elbe-Union already shows a vertical combination having many stages; production of the raw material, such as coal, ore, and limestone; production of intermediary products such as iron and steel; production of semi-manufactured materials such as forged iron, cast-iron, tin, wire, and tubing; production of the finished goods such as tools, screws, rivets, springs, ironwork parts, railway material, and parts for vehicles and ships. This is an excellent example of the vertical system.

The first concern of such a system must be to make sure of its supply of the raw materials, especially of coal. Since the end of the war, coal has acquired a scarcity price. All the factories are fighting for coal. Germany, formerly one of the richest coal-bearing countries, does not possess enough coal fuel for its industries. The distribution is supervised by the State, but it is impossible to keep the factories supplied. The German factories have had to have recourse to the expensive importation of foreign coal. For this reason the Rhine-Elbe-Union has been straining every effort to secure an adequate supply of coal for its factories. The same thing holds good for ores. Where the company has not got enough coal mines in the immediate vicinity, further mines have to be acquired. Since the German-Luxemburg Mining & Smelting Company acquired the Union Company of Dortmund, it has opened several mines in the Dortmund district. As already pointed out, it sought to compensate for its own insufficient coal supply since the war, by combining with the

Gelsenkirchen Mining Company, Inc., and this company in turn found it profitable to enter the combination because this would lead to the extension of the mining business, on account of the blast furnaces of the German-Luxemburg Mining & Smelting Company.

Each individual production stage is built up in relation to the stage above and below it in the cycle of the whole production process. The finished-products factories are assured of the necessary material, while the factories that manufacture the intermediate products are assured of a sufficient coal and ore supply from the stage below, and at the same time can easily dispose of their products to the next stage of manufacture. The geographical concentration also simplifies coöperation and at the same time renders the work less expensive, while the alignment of the various stages of manufacture allows the individual factory to avoid the expensive storage of materials and supplies. This method also avoids the time-robbing selection of materials, the increased cost due to the middle-man, and the uncertainty of getting the right materials.

It is clear that an enterprise of this sort can produce better goods in greater volume, than an isolated factory. The use of its own products, the decrease in its maintenance cost, and its strategic industrial position allow it to grow faster than other enterprises. We are therefore witnessing a concentration race in the German industry of to-day, especially in the mining industry. Only a few large enterprises remain unconsolidated. The old firms of Klöckner, Stumm, Haniel, Funke, Thyssen, Stinnes, and others, are growing into gigantic combinations which are constantly drawing more closely together.

A few months after it was formed, the Rhine-Elbe-Union was enlarged through the acquisition of the Bochum Company, engaged in mining and cast steel manufacturing. This plant, which represents an extensive combination in the Rhine-Westphalian district, has been in existence for sixty years. It includes blast furnaces, steel smelters, foundries, hammer and mill works, and factories for manufacturing railroad material, as well as a large number of subsidiary plants. As many as 18,000 hands are employed. The Company procures the greater part of its raw materials through the operation of its own mines, coke plants, quartz mines, and limestone fields. It also owns a network of iron-ore mines in the ore district bordering on the Sieg River.

Before the Bochum Company joined the Rhine-Elbe-Union it went through a curious experience on the stock exchange. A Berlin banker attempted to buy up the shares of the Bochum Company on the stock exchange, causing a series of fantastic price fluctuations. When this speculator had accumulated a majority control of the Company, he began to look about for a purchaser. The rumor had been spread that foreign interests, taking advantage of the exchange situation, were seeking to acquire the Company. The Bochum Company might easily have shared the fate of the Phönix Company, and other German enterprises. At this point, the Stinnes group decided to acquire the Company despite the artificially high price. A purchase price was agreed upon and the speculation came to an end. The whole episode was an exception rather than the rule, for German industry is rarely subjected to such purely financial operations.

The acquisition of the Bochum Company was of crucial importance to the Rhine-Elbe-Union for perfecting its plan for manufacturing intermediary and finished products. Its negotiations with the refined-steel factory of Böhler Brothers & Company was a step in the same direction.

Mining enterprises lead not only to the metal industries, but to the electrical industry as well. Both of these industries had attracted the attention of Stinnes. He intended the Rhine-Westphalian Electrical Company to supply the two industrial provinces of Rhineland and Westphalia. These two provinces are, of course, thickly studded with innumerable factories, electrical distributing stations, power houses, gas and electrical plants, railroad stations, and trade centres, not to mention hundreds of municipalities, with their network of railroads and street car systems, all of which consume light and power. By 1920 the Company had undergone considerable expansion through the acquisition of power houses and new districts requiring electrical service. Its supply of raw materials was covered by an agreement with the Rhine Lignite Works at the Rodder mine. A further supply of lignite comes from the mines of A. Riebeck in Middle Germany, as well as from the lignite mines in Brunswick.

The Stinnes Trust thus rounded off its mining interests at both ends through its consolidation with the German-Luxemburg

Mining and Smelting Company, and the Gelsenkirchen and Bochum Companies. The next step followed in the same year. In 1920 Hugo Stinnes consolidated his mining business with the Siemens Company in order to form a gigantic electro-mining industry.

The Siemens Company began its career in a small workshop which Werner Siemens started in 1847, in an obscure location in Berlin. From these humble beginnings Siemens and his partner Halske developed a great telegraph and cable construction company. This company built and installed the entire Russian telegraph system. One of the outstanding characteristics of the Siemens family is its love of independence. Thus for example, Werner Siemens for many years opposed the transformation of the firm into a corporation, so that this step was not taken until 1897.

This year marks the beginning of a great development. The company assumed gigantic proportions. The severe panic of

1900, which played havoc with the electrical industry, threatened a number of the larger electrical companies, which had become involved in some very risky ventures. The great electrical company of Siemens and the A. E. G. (Allgemeine Elektrizitäts-Gesellschaft) were the only ones that remained unshaken. The others, in so far as they continued to function at all, had to seek support from these two. At that time the consolidation of the Siemens Company with the Nürnberg Electrical Company (formerly Schuckert & Company) took place. These two companies formed the subsidiary Siemens-Schuckert Company for the purpose of developing methods of high power transmission. A number of other companies were likewise formed in connection with the Siemens enterprise.

The Company supplies a remarkable number of consumers, including electric and gas companies, electric mining plants, and subsidiary railroads of all kinds. Among these are the Franckonian transmission station, the high power houses, Franken and Thüringen; the establishment of Kupferdreh; the distributing station, Südharz; the A. G. Wiener Lokalbahn Co.; the Rhine Electrical Company of Mannheim; the local Berg Railroad; the Hamburg and Stettin Electrical Companies, the electrical street railway systems of Elberfeld, Barmen, Würzburg, and so forth. The Company is also interested in machine and automobile factories, as well as in other factories at home and abroad.

The products of the Siemens Company comprise electrical manufactures and equipments of all sorts, from incandescent lamps to subways. It also manufactures general machinery, fine mechanical and optical instruments, and other instruments of all sorts, as well as automobiles and automobile trucks.

It is noteworthy that the Stinnes Trust, as in the case of the Gelsenkirchen Mining Company, Inc., did not effect the consolidation with the Siemens Company through any financial operation, but through direct negotiations. Mutual necessity and the prospect of joint benefits probably played quite as large a role as the personality of Stinnes and his gift for organizing.

This electro-mining company is called the "Siemens-Rhine-Elbe-Schuckert-Union." This pivotal organization regulates the financial affairs of all the related companies, and works out the plans for a joint administration. But the intention is to keep the management and the administration of each member independent. The object of the consolidation was described as follows, by the chairman of the board of directors of the Siemens-Halske Company: "In these days, where nothing is left to us except intelligent and highly trained workers, we must see to it that everything that we can extract from our soil does not reach the markets of the world until it has been partly or entirely manufactured by our own labor."

This huge company, with its 200,000 employees, is in a position to experiment with power-saving devices, radical innovations, and opportune expansions as well as to introduce methods of specialization and standardization. This is one of the great advantages of concentrated effort.

The consolidation of the Siemens Company with the great mining interests having been effected, it remains for us to follow the further development of its great competitor, the Allgemeine Elektrizitäts-Gesellschaft. Here also we already see the beginning of vertical combination. By virtue of its connections, especially with the Rhine-Westphalian industrial district, which is a large consumer, the Siemens Company will enjoy extraordinary advantages in regard to its supplies as well as the disposal of its products. It is equally certain that the future plans of the Stinnes Trust, which are already looking beyond the boundaries of Germany, will be of the greatest importance for the electrical industry.

In order to round out the company, Stinnes has also begun affiliations with certain metal works such as copper and brass factories, which are of great importance for the electrical industry, and has also become interested in aluminum plants. In addition, he has brought the automobile industry within his sphere, through the purchase of the Loeb automobile factory in Berlin.

According to the agreement, the members of the Siemens-Rhine-Elbe-Schuckert-Union are merged together into a homogeneous organization, to last until the year 2000. The time seems to have arrived when individuals can plan industrial combinations for centuries ahead.

CHAPTER VII

THE Stinnes Trust has grown from the
Rhine-Westphalian industrial district until
it extends over the whole of Germany.
Through the Siemens-Schuckert Company,
it has gained a foothold in the most important industrial cities of Bavaria. At
the time of the consolidation, the combined
directorates made a statement in which
they pointed out the economic and political
importance of this event. They declared
that Bavaria and Berlin are combining
with Rhineland and Westphalia to form a
firmly knit economic unity which is destined to counteract every attempt at separ-
ation. The sentiment of these German
industrial leaders was echoed on another

occasion by the forces of labor. In the summer of 1920, at a conference of labor union delegates from all the mines, a resolution was passed pledging the men to joint action with the labor organizations of the railroads and water highways, to cut off the supply of coal, coke and briquettes from any part of the country which should attempt to secede from Germany.

In view of the weakness of the present German state authority, these economic arguments are of great importance when facing the danger of isolation and secession.

Aside from its success in South Germany, the Stinnes Trust has recently obtained a strong foothold in the most important industrial sections of Prussia. It controls the importation of coal and the coal market, and shares in the distribution of machines and manures for the agricultural operations of East Prussia. It has acquired an almost monopolistic position in the manufacture of cellulose, one of the chief products of this region. All the cellulose factories of

East Prussia, which is rich in forests, are under the Stinnes control.

Hugo Stinnes also turned his attention to German Austria. This country cannot continue to exist for any length of time without a close economic affiliation with an economically strong foreign country. It will soon have to decide in what direction this is to take place. After a long period of paralysis and impotence, German Austria is making frantic efforts to take care of its economic future. The industries are being transformed and are adapting themselves to altered conditions of production. The attempt is being made to replace the antiquated and only partly active factories with modern plants, and to use the country's untapped sources of energy. Austrian territory is being examined for deposits of coal, oil, natural gas, and chemicals.

The severance of the Danube states from Austria, in accordance with the treaty, has caused a number of vital industries to come under foreign jurisdiction. German Austria can no longer count on these nor on any other foreign industries. Her moribund exchange does not permit her to import as formerly, and is allowing foreign countries to buy up Austrian industries to an alarming extent.

Yet, despite her present weakness, Austria is rich in economic possibilities. In Upper Austria, in Salzburg and in the Tyrol, there are coal deposits; oil seems to be present in various localities, and valuable deposits of kaolin, or porcelain-earth, which may form the basis for a highly developed porcelain industry. There are sufficient forests to support a flourishing paper-making industry. The use of water power would put the electrical industry on its feet, and the power thus developed could furnish the entire mechanical energy for industrial and transportation purposes. In the spring of 1921, the Stinnes Trust acquired the Austrian Alpine Mining Company, by buying up the stock. This company owns the Styrian mining deposits, the greatest mine of Europe, and used to play an important part before the war in supplying Italy and the Balkans with iron and steel. In 1916, the best year of the mine, 2,360,000 tons of ore were mined, yielding 637,000 tons of pig iron, and 300,000 tons of rolled steel. After the war, the production was greatly diminished. In 1919 the production had dwindled to 244,000 tons of ore, yielding 59,000 tons of pig iron and 70,000 tons of rolled steel, which represents about one-tenth of the former production.

When things were at their lowest ebb, a Viennese banker bought the majority stock control, and sold the greater part of it, with enormous profit, to an Italian syndicate. This acquisition was of great importance for Italy. The Italian industry, with little iron to fall back upon in its own country, was now in a position to secure its iron supply from Styria. The idea was an excellent one, but conditions made it impossible to carry it out. For Italy, with hardly any coal of its own, could not furnish the necessary coke to refine the ore. The Italians controlled the mine for almost two years without extracting a single ounce of iron.

Besides the lack of coke, the Italian syndicate also faced a lack of labor. Formerly, any amount of Italian laborers were to be had to run the industry, but they now entirely abstained from coming, which is quite natural, since no Italian could be induced to work to-day for wages paid in Austrian crowns. On the other hand, the syndicate was in no position to pay wages in Italian lire.

The Austrian company formerly had obtained the greater part of its coke from its own coke plants in Orlau near Ostrau in Moravia, as well as from other Moravian coke plants, and from the Ruhr coal district. The States that came into existence through the fall of Austria erected trade barriers against each other, so that the deliveries of coke from Czecho-Slovakia also ceased. The deliveries from the German district likewise became small and intermittent. As a result of this situation, the company was compelled to make an extremely unfavorable reciprocal agreement with Czecho-Slovakia, according to which the original Austrian company had to deliver pig iron in exchange for coke. But the coke delivery became so inadequate that six of the seven blast furnaces soon had to be banked.

The acquisition of the enterprise by the Stinnes Trust foreshadows a great change, and is of the greatest importance for the Styrian deposits as well as for the entire problem of the economic reconstruction of German Austria. The Stinnes Trust, which controls 15.8% of the entire coal production of Rhine-Westphalia, and 13% of its entire coke output, is in a position to supply all the coke necessary to run the blast furnaces at full capacity, the annual coke requirement being 600,000 tons. The increased production of pig iron is of vital importance in reviving the industries which depend upon iron. Under this arrangement the iron produced at the Styrian mines no longer has ·to be taken to Czecho-Slovakia, but is manufactured right in the country. This means a resumption of the Austrian iron industry, so that it can satisfy the home demand, and at the same time resume the export of iron. The exceptional quality of Styrian iron has played an important part in handicapping Austrian iron manufactures. The iron imported after the closing down of the mine was not always of the quality which the Austrian industries required for their high grade steel products. With the Styrian iron once more at their command, they are now again in a position to supply the market with goods of standard quality.

Hugo Stinnes has been criticized in some quarters for acquiring the Alpine Mining Company. The transaction occurred in the critical days of the London conference. The purchase required large financial resources and was looked upon as a measure calculated to increase the difficulty of an understanding. It may very well be that the impression made in London was not very favorable, but the loss of the ore deposits would certainly have been a much greater calamity. This loss was actually threatened because negotiations with foreign purchasers had already begun, as in the case of the Bochum Company where the stock was almost bought up by foreign investors.

Austria would not have been in a position to put this gigantic mining enterprise into operation again without outside help. The *Kölnische Zeitung*, (the leading paper of Cologne), discussed the importance of the case, in relation to the economic strangulation of Germany and Austria, as follows:

"The post-war policy of the Entente is severely handicapping German industry, and is excluding it from the world market wherever possible. It is transforming Austria-Hungary into a heap of wreckage, and is paralyzing Upper Silesia to the point of industrial impotence. The Entente has abandoned the utterly helpless Balkans, and has nothing to contribute to the reconstruction of Central Europe except insensate reparation demands, penalties, and reprisals. It has converted the 'urge to the southeast' which it formerly falsely ascribed to us, into an irresistible pressure. An enterprising man like Stinnes, whose foresight and largeness of conception even his enemies will not deny, is taking a leap into the dark with the hope of transforming one of the greatest enterprises of the continent into an active member of European industry. The capital involved is no trifle even for Stinnes, and the risk is proportionately large. Yet this step has brought down the wrath of the Entente upon Stinnes, though none moved a finger as long as exploiters from every country in the world tried to share in the auctioning off of Austria. When we consider that Italy, a former ally, had the first chance, but was not able to accomplish anything, and that Schneider-Creusot, made wiser by unfortunate experiences in the case of the Skoda works, left the field open to German industry, it is really hard to see how Stinnes deserves any reproach. The Entente's policy of economic encirclement of Germany cannot ignore the fact that there are limits to these destructive tendencies."

The acquisition of the Alpine Mining Company by the Stinnes Trust has thus far been the only practical step towards the union of Austria and Germany, and has caused a great stir in German Austria. This is brought out in an open letter which a Viennese journalist at that time addressed to Stinnes. He wrote as follows:

"You have attempted to revive the stricken economic condition of German Austria with your financial resources, and have found the point at which the greatest returns may be expected. Why was this step so long in coming? We on the German Austrian side have been indefatigable for over two years in invoking the aid of German capital. There must have been political difficulties, for the economic advantages to both sides were obvious to everybody. But the Italian purchasers could not meet the costs. They probably hoped that their participation in the Alpine Mining Company would induce the Czecho-Slovaks to deliver the coke necessary for the smelting of the Styrian ore in larger quantities, after they had revengefully denied it to the German Austrians. But the Czecho-Slovaks were not to be disturbed in the further enjoyment of their revenge, so that six of seven blast furnaces of the company remained cold. And at that time French, English and American allied interests would not furnish coke, except at exorbitant prices. The result was that the Italians soon lost their enthusiasm for a piece of property which they had so triumphantly acquired.

"You, Mr. Stinnes, are the right substitute for them. For you have what they lacked, namely, coal and coke. It is probable that the thirst for vengeance will now also rapidly disappear among the Czecho-

Slovaks, as was the case in the sugar business, when Austria began to receive sugar from far off Java, at a cheaper price than that which their Czecho-Slovak neighbors' were asking for it. Subsequently, the price of sugar in the world markets declined to such an extent that the Czecho-Slovak sugar could not be sold anywhere at their asking price. Let us hope that the same thing will happen with their coke. They will undoubtedly offer it to the Alpine Mining Company, so that the Westphalian coke will not have to be taken away from German industry. Next, the unemployment will decrease. More hands will be required in order to mine larger quantities of iron-ore, which will also have to be smelted, after which the iron will be used in the factories to manufacture machines, girders, rails, tools, and other articles. The increased supply will cause the price of iron manufactures to come down. This will be followed by a general reduction of prices and wages. Then there will be a gradual resumption of building activity, which will stimulate industry all along the line. In short, the industrial paralysis will cease, and our economic life will again have a healthy circulation.

"For this reason, Mr. Stinnes, the Austrian press is again suddenly favorable to you. This is true even of the Social-Democratic papers which have recently swung back to capitalism. The Social-Democratic party, as you know, has been in a repentant mood ever since the complete collapse of their ambitious socialization plans at the recent congress of the metal workers' unions in Vienna. The Social-Democratic faction in our national parliament is keeping close watch, and has made an interpellation in parliament, drawing the government's attention to the possibility of your shipping the Styrian ore to Germany, and thus paralyzing the Austrian iron industry. But this probably merely caused you to smile, since you are after profits which will be greatest if you have the raw material manufactured as much as possible on the spot, instead of first shipping it to some distant point.

"You must also have been highly amused when one of our reactionary yellow journals expressed the opinion that you had acquired the stocks of the Alpine Mining Company for the sole purpose of shutting down the works for the benefit of the German iron industry. This was undoubtedly a case of deliberately sowing suspicion for some ulterior motive. For you would have much preferred the Italians to keep the stocks of the Company, instead of selling them to you, just as you are shedding no tears over the increasing amount of foreign holdings in Austrian banks and industries, on the part of Frenchmen, Englishmen, and Americans. Let them all continue to acquire such holdings. Those of us who desire the reconstruction of Austria, and her close coöperation with Germany, welcome this foreign participation.".

The step which Hugo Stinnes had thus

taken is fraught with great risk, for he has
invested a gigantic sum and will have to
put still more money into this mining enterprise in order to put it into complete running order. The speculation that preceded
this step will make it extremely difficult to
derive any profit from this huge investment,
but it is characteristic of Hugo Stinnes to
build his business without always having in
mind the question of immediate or early
profit.

While taking these steps in the south and
the east, Stinnes was thinking of still
further ways of keeping open the economic
gates of Germany. Some time before the
war, he had already entered into complicated negotiations for the purpose of connecting his enterprises with foreign sources
of raw materials and foreign fields of consumption. His purpose was to have a cen-
tralized enterprise, producing its own raw
materials for its own transportation lines,
and marketing its wares through its own

merchandising system. In 1920 he added an extensive exporting department to the Hugo Stinnes Transportation and Overseas Trading Company, organized in 1917, to which reference has already been made.

The charter of this company in the commercial register of Hamburg is very interesting. It shows how the varied enterprises of Hugo Stinnes are to be developed. The business is licensed to engage in the following activities: To engage in transportation of every description, as well as to build and manufacture all shipping accessories, whether at home or abroad; to deal in the products of the mining, smelting, and metal industries, the chemical and electrical industry, and agriculture; to market articles of every stage of manufacture, as well as raw materials of all kinds, especially provisions and cattle products, mineral, animal and vegetable oils, cotton, and other textiles in the unfinished state, hides, jute, wood, cellulose, paper, and all products of the intermediate industries; to engage in the re-shipping and storage of all these products, especially during their transmission from or to foreign countries. The company is also licensed to undertake the extraction, manufacture, and construction of every form of raw material and manufactured article in its own establishments.

It is difficult to imagine a more comprehensive industrial organization. Stinnes now proceeds from the mining and electrical business, to become active in the most varied forms of German business enterprise. The Hamburg Travelers Company, which Stinnes founded, together with the Hamburg American Line, enters the field of travel and hotel and health resort management. Steamer cabins, railroad compartments, hotels, and health resorts are unified into one system. The company owns the Esplanade Hotel in Berlin, and the hotels in Oberhof, Thuringia, which are run through the Hotel Management Company, Limited, of Thuringia. These enterprises correlate the varied possibilities of the traveling and tourist business, and open up the prospect of world travel as an organized enterprise. The route from the North Sea to Central Germany, into Switzerland and down to the Mediterranean, is likely to be developed first.

CHAPTER VIII

STINNES AND THE NEWSPAPERS

THERE was much astonishment in Germany when it became known that Hugo Stinnes, the industrial leader, had gone into the newspaper business. His first step was to acquire the well-known *Deutsche Allgemeine Zeitung*. Stinnes is by no means the first German industrial leader to own a newspaper. It is pretty well established that a number of German newspaper properties, advertising concerns, and news bureaus, are under the control of the major industries. The exact connections are not always clear. This state of affairs reflects upon the whole German newspaper system. In many organs of public opinion, it is true, the reader can easily form his opinion of the influence at work behind a newspaper. But in many cases even an experienced person would find difficulty in doing this. The policy of a newspaper may furnish no clew whatsoever, so that it is only by accident that the identity of those in control is discovered. This tendency has gone so far that there are now newspaper proprietors who possess a whole string of different publications, with widely different policies towards political and economic questions. These papers have become pure business enterprises, where it is quite immaterial to those in control whether the paper represents this or that shade of public opinion. These proprietors look upon newspapers solely from the point of view of profit.

Nowadays, another development can occasionally be observed. Men formerly engaged exclusively in the newspaper and advertising business suddenly become interested in branches of industry that are entirely removed from the newspaper business.

Nevertheless, Hugo Stinnes seems to present a special case. The policies of those papers that are demonstrably under his control in no way suggest that Hugo Stinnes is anxious to launch any propaganda in favor of his political or economic point of view. Deeds and not words reveal his influence. It is just possible that he bought these newspapers with the idea of influencing the press in his favor, and winning some of his prospective opponents over to his side. But this is very unlikely.

Up to the present, the operations of Stinnes in this field greatly resemble his coal and electric enterprises. In both cases he proceeds from an economic and practical point of view. The connecting link between his newspapers and his coal business is wood. We have already pointed out that he had acquired extensive forest reserves in order to assure a supply of mining tim-

ber. The possession of so much wood
seems to have suggested the production
cycle from wood pulp to newspapers, according to the vertical system. This as-
sumption is strengthened when one sees
how he has fitted the various stages of production between wood and newspapers into
his enterprises. He owns factories for the
manufacture of cellulose and paper, and
has acquired various cellulose factories at
the headquarters for the raw material in
East Prussia. It is interesting to observe
that he has, at the same time, made use of
his coal companies in order to make sure
of having an uninterrupted supply of coal
from the Ruhr basin for these factories in
East Prussia. In the next stage of paper
manufacturing, Stinnes is likewise in a
position to fit his own plants into the
cycle. It is rumored that the Hugo Stinnes
Book and Cellulose Company is seeking to
acquire control in a number of paper factories. His acquisition of the large Büx-
enstein Printing Company of Berlin and

the North German Book Binding and Publishing Company, paves the way to the next step in the paper industry. The whole enterprise culminates in the newspapers which Stinnes has already bought. Here we may again observe the same economic cycle from the raw product through the intermediate product to the finished article, all under the same uniform administration, as in the case of the other enterprises of the Stinnes Trust.

The business efficiency of Stinnes makes it seem probable that he will also attempt to bring his newspapers to the highest possible stage of technical and administrative perfection. Nevertheless the *Deutsche Allgemeine Zeitung* is still far from being a journal of distinction, comparable let us say, to the French *Matin*. It also lacks the millions of readers who support newspapers of such world - wide circulation. Judged from appearances only, it is true, the *Deutsche Allgemeine Zeitung* is the greatest

German newspaper. But the modest circulation among small officials which this fussy little paper formerly enjoyed, as well as under the excellent management of the deceased Mr. Hobbing, has remained the same. Editorial offices and experts value it as before for its information service, but the paper has no influence on any larger sections of the public. With all his newspaper purchases, Stinnes is still far from being a Lord Northcliffe, and probably has no intention of becoming one.

The report that Stinnes has already purchased sixty German papers seems to be largely exaggerated. The number probably does not exceed a dozen or so.

The danger of a trustification of the press certainly has possibilities which must not be underestimated. Powerful personalities might easily use their economic control of the press in order to sway public opinion in certain definite directions, and to misuse their influence. It is a matter for legislation to be beforehand in checking the dangers that might result from such a trustification, with its attendant concealment of the nature of the control behind newspapers.

CHAPTER IX

STINNES IN THE PUBLIC EYE

SINCE the war, Germany has had to fight for its very existence. This struggle is taking place primarily in the field of economics. Formerly, losing a war entailed the loss of territory or the complete loss of political independence, whereas to-day the consequences of such a war are a confiscation of goods; these goods are either taken out of the defeated country in the form of raw materials or finished products, or else the same result is accomplished by curtailing the conquered country's share in the world's trade and commerce, in favor of the victors.

For a long time the coal question remained in the foreground of the peace negotiations. France had lost enormous quantities of this important raw material through the war. It will take years before the French coal mines can be brought back to their former output. This explains why France was so interested in putting the demand for German coal deliveries into the forefront of the discussion. But even a half-way informed opponent must have recognized the absolute impossibility of meeting the demand for the enormous amount of almost 40,000,000 tons of coal, as stipulated in the treaty of peace. At the time not even a quarter of this amount could be delivered. It is true that the output of coal from the Ruhr basin increased considerably in 1919 and 1920. But it was still insufficient to supply German industry with the necessary fuel.

The hostile powers saw that Germany could not be compelled to deliver the amount of coal demanded, by means of any peremptory command. Since the days of San Remo, they seemed to realize that the only possible way of arriving at a real repar-

ation programme was by resorting to negotiations. There followed the conference at
Spa, which began with a fair prospect of
arriving at a European understanding,
though this promise ultimately failed to
be realized.

The negotiations took place in the Villa
Fraineuse, the former seat of the imperial
headquarters. The French delegates seemed
unable to dispense with the florid rhetoric
which characterizes so many French political utterances. The German delegates
were in an extraordinarily difficult position.
The amount of coal demanded of them was
so large that they did not wish to take the
responsibility of accepting it without further authorization. They therefore summoned the German experts to Spa in order
to hear their opinions. Hugo Stinnes was
accordingly summoned to Spa to testify as
an expert.

Opinion among the German delegates
was divided. On the one hand they were
threatened with the occupation of the

Ruhr basin, but on the other hand, they were frightened by the prospect for German industry which such an exhaustion of Germany's raw materials seemed to open up before them. Hugo Stinnes anticipated such catastrophic results from accepting the demand of the Entente, that he used the entire force of his personality and his prestige as an expert to insist upon a refusal. The delegates decided to let Stinnes present his arguments personally, at a plenary sitting of the conference. Mr. Hué, representing the German miners, was also present as an expert, and was equally convinced of the serious consequences of the loss of coal to Germany, and appeared before the conference at this same sitting as the representative of the German coal miners in order to state the grounds for his adverse opinion.

Stinnes insisted that it would be absolutely impossible to make an annual delivery of 40,000,000 tons. He recognized the pressing need of France for reparation coal, but considered that even the preliminary delivery of 2,000,000 tons per month could not be carried out for the present. A few days before, he had already made a similar declaration to a representative of the French press. In this interview, he stated that he considered the Spa conference to be premature, and likely to turn out a failure for both parties concerned. He was in favor of allowing these economic and social questions to mature for several months, believing that many of them would ultimately solve themselves. He further believed that Germany would, in the course of time, be able to increase its labor efficiency, and that it was ready at any time for international coöperation.

Stinnes referred particularly to the possibility of coöperation between France and Germany. The fact that the two countries were adjacent was a direct invitation to carry out the necessary reconstruction together, and to satisfy their economic needs on the basis of mutual understanding. But he looked upon Spa as still enveloped in an atmosphere of mutual suspicion.

The arguments of Stinnes before the conference were heard with the greatest attention. The delegates saw before them the representative of German industry, who rejected the gestures of diplomacy and dealt with sharp-edged realities. The speech of Mr. Hué strengthened this impression. These speeches marked a departure in the proceedings of these political negotiations. The momentary effect, it is true, was not very great. The guiding stars of the French and English statesmen were not economic but political. It was made evident that a memorandum or an expert opinion, no matter how carefully and thoroughly composed, makes little impression upon men of the stamp of Briand and Lloyd George, who are even likely to dismiss it without further consideration. This method of presenting the German arguments was out of place, at least as far as any immediate results are to be expected.

HUGO STINNES

Mr. John Maynard Keynes, the English expert, was entirely right in his pessimism about Spa. He expected no insight from Spa that would do justice to the realities of the situation. At the time of the conference at Spa, the coal question was no longer an economic issue, as far as the French delegate was concerned, but a political one. If Millerand had failed to satisfy the French public, his political career would have ended. England on the other hand, having in mind certain political steps in Asia Minor, for which it was necessary to gain French approval, was compelled to hold back from any practical discussion. The demands of France were put through to the accompaniment of the military threats of Marshal Foch.

The utterly impractical nature of the reparation negotiations is revealed by the fact that France already has an over-supply of coal, despite the fact that the German coal deliveries are far from reaching the amount demanded at Spa. At the same time, the reconstruction work is being held up. A distribution of German effort, so as to meet the actual varied requirements of France, would not have hampered Germany as much as these coal deliveries, and would have been of much greater benefit to France. The French economic body just now resembles an organism which has been stuffed to the bursting point with undigestible nourishment.

The attitude of Hugo Stinnes at Spa was afterwards sharply criticized in Germany. He was accused of having made such a curt refusal with the deliberate intention of bringing about the occupation of the Ruhr basin. It was alleged that this would have meant no diminution of his profits. It was also hinted that he wanted the Ruhr basin to be in French hands, in order to escape the German socialization schemes. The answer to this is that Stinnes certainly could have found other and less dangerous alternatives if his actions had really been determined by mere

considerations of profit or the fear of socialization. At the same time it must be said
that Stinnes seemed to be of the opinion
that the French would in the course of
time undoubtedly find some excuse for oc-
cupying the Ruhr basin. As he explained
later in justifying his conduct at Spa, he
considered that the results would have
been less harmful for the future of Germany
if the occupation had taken place immediately at the time of the Spa conference,
rather than now or later.

The conference at Spa was preceded by
an interview between Stinnes and Miller-
and. The foreign press reported that
Stinnes had outlined a plan of close coöperation between the French and German
coal and iron industries, which was to be
of the greatest importance in the upbuilding
of German economic life. His plan was
supposed to have been worked out to the
most minute detail. It was said to have
made a strong impression in France, but
that the French industrial leaders had op-

posed Stinnes' proposal. It was probably feared that such a coöperation would work out to the detriment of French industry on account of the superior organization of German industries.

The pessimistic calculations of Stinnes in regard to the coal deliveries have turned out to be untrue. The figures were probably correct, but evolution has shown that a vital organism is elastic enough to form new growths where the old growth has been cut off. Nevertheless it is true that the experiment was never carried out according to the figures which Stinnes had in mind. The insufficient output, despite extra shifts, subsidies, and an increased number of laborers, on Germany's part, and the transportation difficulties of France, have made it impossible to carry out completely the agreement at Spa.

The common sense harmony between employers and employees revealed at Spa, made a deep impression upon the public both in Germany and abroad. But the effect of this soon disappeared in Germany, when political and labor dissensions broke out with unprecedented severity immediately after the occurrences at Spa. The attacks upon Stinnes came thick and fast. Among other things, he was accused of seeking to acquire influence in France in order to limit German prerogatives in the Ruhr basin, and to split labor by means of his newspapers. A letter which Hugo Stinnes wrote to one of the men who attacked him, is of considerable interest. In July, 1920, he wrote as follows:

"I find that you have made certain prominent statements in the *Arbeiterzeitung*[1] of Essen to which I am replying because they have been made by a man who is a member of our own mining industry, and because these statements, unless they are contradicted, are likely to cause mischief in our mining community. The experts of the coal industry, present at Spa, had

---

[1] A newspaper devoted to the interests of labor published in Essen.

two objects in mind when they made their
fight to keep the compulsory deliveries of
coal to the hostile Entente within certain
limits. They wanted first to save the German mining unions from having to do a
great amount of overtime work at a period
when their food supply was inadequate.
In the second place they did not want the
unions to assume the responsibility for an
even greater increase of unemployment and
want in all other industries.

In the discussions of the socialization
commission, and in the committee of the
State Economic Council, I called particular attention to the fact that, contrary to
many of my associates, I did not take the
stand that the abolition of the eight-hour
day could be looked upon as a cure-all to
remedy the present depression within what
might be called a reasonable time. It is
therefore outrageous of you to accuse me
of having taken the opposite position. The
only correct statement you make is that I
declared that overtime work was essential

to change the present conditions in the departments of mining, agriculture, and transportation. What you say about a French-German Purchasing Company, in Paris, in which I am supposed to be heavily interested, is either a careless or a deliberate misrepresentation on your part. For it has been constantly emphasized that only the German unions and the Coal Syndicate were to benefit from this French-German Purchasing Company. This was again brought out at the recent congress of mining unions. If it is your intention to create a dissension and suspicion between employers and employees in the coal mining industry, whether through ignorance of the facts, or deliberately, you are merely furthering the interests of our common oppressors, with the result that the Rhine-Westphalian miners will have to drudge like slaves for foreign masters for years to come, to the great detriment of Germany. You will thus do the same harm as a number of our representatives at Spa, who through racial bias, broke down German resistance against degrading demands. I hope that you will see to it that my reply to your statements is conspicuously printed in the *Arbeiterzeitung*. Good luck to you!"

Hugo Stinnes had every right to repudiate such suspicions. An expert called in to give his opinion must be allowed to state his case frankly, without being suspected of bad motives. On this occasion, it is true, Stinnes exposed himself by ascribing motives inspired by racial bias to other experts who did not share his point of view. Perhaps he wanted to defend himself against the impression which a French newspaper had created, by describing Stinnes as having a Semitic appearance. On this occasion Stinnes had been characterized as "half a professor, half a rabbi." In any case, Stinnes' attack upon his associates at Spa was most unfortunate.

Since Spa, Stinnes has been especially down on politicians. After the negotiations at the London Conference, he made a sharp attack upon the German conduct of the negotiations, in the Committee on Foreign Affairs of the German parliament. He reproached the Cabinet for having a foreign policy that was without any guiding idea or fixed plan. Lately, an interview of Stinnes has been republished, which he is supposed to have given to a foreign correspondent.

"We are merely losing time through the chatter of politicians who are wound up like automatons by parliament and the newspapers. What we need is a conference of business men who can talk to each other without hate. There must be no more conferences at which everybody lays down his revolver at his side. This sick world can only be saved by a consultation of a few physicians behind closed doors. It would be insane on the part of Germany to declare its willingness to pay even the interest on a loan of 50,000,000,000 marks. If the Allies are figuring on any such sums, they are going to have another disappoint-

ment. France could have had material
and labor for construction two years ago,
and no German would have refused to deliver them. France, however, was not
really interested in reparation, but was
seeking to humiliate Germany. At the
present moment there are only two kinds of
countries in the world—those which can
buy raw materials because of the state of
exchange, and those which can not do this.
Both are bound to perish unless some form
of coöperation can be agreed upon. Money
is to be found, but only by giving the world
an example of perfect coöperation. Every
business man knows that money is to be
had, only the politicians do not seem to
know it. I am trying to save my country
from destruction, and at the same time save
the other countries."

This interview is without doubt essentially correct. For this is the way Stinnes
thinks and speaks. He is always terse and
sure of himself, and sees things in a large
way, though he is sometimes a little reck-

less. It is certain that Stinnes will make use of his whole organizing power to solve European problems when the time comes. It is not like him to stand aside and sulk.

As a party man, Stinnes belongs to the German People's Party (Volkspartei). The party seems to have entertained the hope that this powerful trust magnate would make a strong foundation for a political platform. These expectations have not been realized. Hugo Stinnes seems to have no desire to substitute a form of narrowly conceived and unprofitable party politics for his industrial activity.

Stinnes has lately been severely taken to task for launching three ships which were christened with somewhat opprobrious names. To call these three ships "Hindenburg," "Tirpitz," and "Ludendorff," was looked upon as a provocation, though it is not likely that this idea ever entered his mind. For the construction of these ships had been begun at a period when these three names still sounded differently to Germans, than they now do. The three men in question had probably agreed to act as godfathers for the ships some time ago. It would have been very surprising if a man like Stinnes had allowed any psychological or tactical considerations to influence him to change the names of the ships at the last moment.

CHAPTER X

COAL and iron are the foundations of German industry. He who controls them controls the smallest business. By producing,
manufacturing, and exporting them, Germany can exchange goods with the industries of the world; she can satisfy her own
needs and make enough profit to increase
and improve the supply; she can put her
factories into more and more perfect condition. Mr. Vögler, one of the directors of
the Stinnes Trust, is quite right when he
says: "With us the potato has long ago become a product of coal."

For this reason the question of creating
new economic systems always involves the
control of coal and iron. Newspapers, pub-

lic meetings, and commissions have long been engrossed in plans for the development of these new systems. Germany was the first country to create a State Economic Council, a parliamentary institution created for the purpose of taking economic questions out of the hands of politically divided parties, and giving them to competent representatives of the various trades and professions to evolve some suitable working basis.

In the State Economic Council, representatives of every occupation come together for practical work on these economic questions. After the events at Spa in 1920, the question of socializing the mines was exhaustively discussed. The records of the proceedings read like an exciting drama which shows the conflict of opinions and interests on a broad stage, not without an occasional bit of satire.

In the debate over the socialization of the mines, there was found to be a sharp conflict of opinion. Hugo Stinnes, who belongs to the State Economic Council, took an active part in the discussions. When the first negotiations failed to establish a common basis, the so-called "Committee of Understanding" was formed, which proceeded from Berlin to Essen, into the heart of the coal district, in order to arrive at some practical results. Besides Stinnes and Vögler, this committee included a number of other employers and employees from the various branches of the coal industry, and the series of factories belonging to the next stage of manufacturing. This meeting at Essen resulted in an expert's memorandum which was essentially the work of Stinnes. The other large industrial leaders of German industries subscribe to the collectivist point of view contained in this memorandum. As we cannot digress too far into the details of these proposals, we shall limit ourselves to elaborating upon the two most important ones.

The memorandum declares itself in favor

of creating vertical consolidations of the
industry. The object is to utilize the raw
materials to the greatest possible extent,
and to manufacture them into finished
products as efficiently as possible. When
these various vertical combinations within
the industry have brought about the greatest possible economic concentration, they
are to be organized in relation to each
other on the horizontal system. The whole
industry will then be trustified both vertically and horizontally into a collective
unit. This will ensure the maximum service, and will thus fulfill one of the main
demands of socialistic organization. According to Stinnes, trustification and socialization run parallel, and do not have to
intersect each other. The second proposal
is to create industrial provinces. The economic field is to be divided, not according
to geographical and political relations, but
strictly according to a practical economic
point of view. Within every uniform district there will be a combination of all

the branches of industry, and a joint regulation of power production, raw material output, and manufacturing, together with the necessary transportation facilities. In forming these industrial provinces, Stinnes is developing a plan which he had already tried to put into practice before the war. Both his mining establishments in the Ruhr district, and his development of the electrical business, had been planned with the idea of creating a uniform industrial district. To carry out this form of collectivism, Stinnes also proposes to have the employees hold shares in the industry.

These lines of development have been evolved from practical experience, and follow out the purpose which Stinnes had in mind in establishing his enterprises and consolidating the various branches into his Trust. The importance of these consolidations for the economic development of Germany is indisputable. The proposal of minor stock participation is not essential to the development of collectivism, and may even become an impediment. The participation of the individual employee in the enterprises would merely strengthen economic individualism. Other business men demanded the participation of the employees as a form of collectivism. Socialization itself has thus far made little progress. The great unknown quantities, which the unsolved reparations problem has called forth, must first be eliminated from world economics. No amount of negotiation so far has even succeeded in reducing these quantities to practical dimensions.

Until this is done it is not very likely that a transformation of the present-day economic system can be accomplished through legislation. In this connection, it is interesting to hear the opinion of French Socialists about the economic system which Stinnes has created. A short time ago *Le Peuple* pointed out how this concentration had cheapened production and avoided the waste of raw material, and referred to this form of organization as "a step which France might well imitate." French industry, this newspaper continued, had found nothing better to do than to raise the tariff. This merely stunted business initiative and diminished competition in world economics, whereas these German concentrations had not only proved that production methods could be improved but had shown how such improvements could be made.

CHAPTER XI

THE SIGNIFICANCE OF STINNES IN GERMAN ECONOMIC DEVELOPMENT

THERE is no doubt about the strength of Stinnes' personality. But it is equally certain that from an economic point of view he is rapidly growing beyond a mere personality: he is becoming his own work.

The Stinnes Trust serves as a model illustration of German trustification. This differs in many ways from the well-known American trust, in respect to its origins, its development, and its results. The untapped natural resources of America offered unprecedented opportunities for profit to the trusts. In Germany, on the other hand, there were already large numbers of independent business men who had sprung

up as a result of the division and utilization
of the country's deposits of raw materials,
and the advanced technical development;
so that a trust could not be formed except
through a combination of individual daring
and an extraordinary gift for organization.
American trust builders also have frequently
made clever use of the stock exchange operations, in order to gain control of various
enterprises. Large scale speculations of
this sort have been rare occurrences in Germany. It is only quite recently that the
stock exchanges of Berlin and Vienna have
witnessed such sensational operations. They
will cease as soon as the exchange has been
stabilized.

The German concentration movement
did not take place primarily through financial operations, but through logical consolidations of enterprises that were at the
same stage of manufacture, or were engaged
in similar manufacturing processes. Such
consolidations offered great advantages in
the running of the business, which did not

exist in the case of isolated enterprises. They led to economy and skill in the purchase of raw materials, and where they were built up on the basis of their own raw materials, this feature frequently put them in the favorable position of being able to procure their material without expensive middle-men's costs, and without time-robbing and costly transportation. They could also regulate the production of raw materials according to whatever standard of quality they required.

The special forms of industrial organizations peculiar to mining were to the advantage of factories that handled several processes at different stages. The protracted dissensions in the Rhine-Westphalian Coal Syndicate had resulted from the fact that a large number of mining industries, as well as factories involving several processes, were members of the same syndicates and cartels. The cartel form of business organization will probably disappear entirely.

An essential difference between German

and American trusts also lies in the fact, that in America the domination of the trust in most cases led to the complete control of an entire industrial field. Thus the all-powerful Standard Oil Company, whose history is associated with the name of Rockefeller, completely dominated the American oil industry within the short space of ten years after it had absorbed 39 competing companies. At one time it transported and distributed 95% of the entire American production. Germany had no such example of monopoly because a number of equally powerful trusts grew up within the same branch of industry. When the period of consolidation approached, German industry had numerous large enterprises with a highly developed individuality. At present, the mining industry alone includes a number of large firms. So far no single trust dominates. As a result the head of every trust is stimulated to make a maximum effort. No mining trust can afford to rely upon its powerful position, and to let up in its effort to perfect its equipment and to increase its production. This continually forces German trusts to do everything in their power to try to cheapen production costs and to extract the maximum effort from their workmen.

Another trait of the German trusts is the principle of federation basis on which they are organized, corresponding to the characteristics of the German people. As the Stinnes Trust shows, decentralization is the very thing aimed at, so as to preserve and increase the independence of the individual enterprises and the pride of each director in his responsibility, as well as to avoid stagnation in the office management and in the shop.

Germany to-day shows the most diversified forms of consolidations in every field. But they all have the same object in common, namely, to organize industry on a more rational basis. This is essential in order to keep Germany alive. The fact that this process is taking place from within is a sign of inner vitality. To what this development will lead later on, cannot yet be foreseen. Theories differ in regard to the efficiency of these concentrations. The dispute between the partisans of these theories frequently takes violent forms. But in the meantime the development goes steadily on. Germany must of course prevent unhealthy excrescences of this development. But the development itself is bound to take place.

The importance of German trusts for the future of Germany is certainly very great. So-called normal economic conditions, in the period before the war, now seem almost mediæval and provincial. The development is taking place with enormous rapidity. The pressure of conditions from without, the actual or threatened loss of vital industrial sections, and the prohibition of export and import, would necessarily have destroyed Germany if unsuspected forces had not been liberated and been made to unfold from within. Germany will become a sparsely settled agricultural state unless the formation of new kinds of economic organization can bring about greater, better, and cheaper production. Trusts induce and facilitate the growth of these new economic organizations. It is worth while to observe the effects of trustification in the case of the Stinnes Trust.

The consolidation of the Gelsenkirchen Mining Company Inc. with the German-Luxemburg Mining & Smelting Company and the Bochum Company, combines a large number of similar plants engaged in the production of coal, iron-ore, limestone, and dolomite. These raw materials are extracted not only for the factories belonging to the trust, but to a considerable extent for outside factories as well. This combination makes it possible to employ cheaper and better methods of extraction because the joint management eliminates competition, and facilitates a better organized plan of distribution. The expenses of the Trust are also reduced through the manufacture of its own raw materials. The factories are thereby put in a position to invest much more money in new enterprises where the results may be doubtful, than isolated establishments which operate much closer to the profit and loss margin. Innovations of a technical nature can also be introduced with much less risk.

The by-products and intermediary products of the mining industry can be utilized to the greatest advantage. Here also the history of the Stinnes Trust shows that a number of technical innovations were made possible only by distributing the risk of the experiment over the individual factories. By-products such as coke and lime can be manufactured in the company's own factories in any grade or quality desired. The Trust can obtain all the necessary materials for the production of pig iron from its own plants, and the smelting takes place in its own establishments. Steel of every grade, cast-iron, blast furnace cement, and slag stones, are all produced according to the needs of the factories at the next stages of manufacture.

Semi-manufactured products of every form and quality are successively produced by a chain of related factories. The establishments at Gelsenkirchen produce railroad material, bar iron, tin, and tubing; the Bochum Company manufactures railroad material, forged iron, bar iron, and cast iron. The Brüninghaus factories produce crude forged iron and bar iron; the former works at Thomée produce bar iron and rolled steel wire. The former independent works at Berg manufacture bar iron, various forms of tin, wire, and tubing; the German-Luxemburg Mining & Smelting Company manufactures railroad material, forged iron, cast-iron, tins and wires. The affiliated factories of the Siemens Company also produce bar iron and wire.

The finished products of the German-Luxemburg Company include all kinds of tools, screws and rivets, springs, forged parts, switches, railroad and bridge construction material, cranes, cables, railroad and street cars, freight cars, machines and ships. The Company obtains all its necessary materials for these manufacturing processes from the series of factories engaged in the production of intermediary products. The Bochum Company depends upon previous production stages of the industry for its manufacture of forgings and railroad material.

This foundation of raw material, semi- and finished product, serves the Siemens Company for the manufacture of the most varied articles. These include: generators, motors, transformers, switchboards, material for installations, cables and conduits, telegraph and telephone apparatus, signal apparatus, measuring instruments, electro-medial apparatus, hydrometers, railroad safety devices, trucks and automobiles, artificial coal, porcelain and paper for technical purposes, incandescent lamps, electrical distributing stations, electrical equipment for industrial power plants, for electrical transportation, and for chemical industries; long distance telephone apparatus and transmission equipment, signal and switchboard equipment, and underground and hydraulic building material.

Beginning at the bottom of the scale, every stage of manufacture is undertaken in relation to the stage next above, so that the raw material is gradually transformed into a finished product of the best possible quality. Whenever changes in the finished product are called for, suitably equipped factories can be installed at any of the preliminary stages of manufacture.

The divisions in this system are not rigid. Horizontal and vertical combinations parallel and intersect each other. Many industries are divided vertically or horizontally within themselves, and some are connected with others both horizontally and vertically. Every stage of manufacture, besides having its place in the production scale as a whole, is itself minutely organized. This rational systematizing of factories will undoubtedly be developed still further. This combination is of especial importance in the case of factories that are connected in a series. The horizontal division, which economic experts have been insisting upon, is therefore already fore-shadowed in the Stinnes Trust, and will probably be further developed.

Stinnes is generally regarded as the strongest exponent of the vertical trust. The most recent developments show that even those industrial leaders who formerly were the strongest opponents of vertical trusts can no longer get along without the expansion of their enterprises both upward and downward in the scale of production. A combination of the vertical and the horizontal systems will probably take place to a very great extent in the near future.

The Stinnes Trust has been very much attacked. In most cases the attack is not against Stinnes himself but against the form of trustification, so that it also applies to other large trusts which are being formed in Germany. The point is being made that the development of these trusts is not organic but is due to the tremendous pressure of external circumstances. In case of a return to a period of normal economic activity in the future, it is considered very dangerous to have these trusts absorb a large number of major and minor industries which they will no longer be able to utilize when conditions are stablized again. But after the factories are either abandoned or closed down, it will still be necessary to pay off both interest and principal on the large amounts of capital invested. This necessity will form an undesirable liability which must be charged against prices. The same reasoning applies to the overpayments which are often being made to-day in acquiring new properties. These liabilities will prevent price reduction, and will finally be passed on to the consumer, so that the people as a whole will suffer economic harm.

It is also claimed that there is great

danger of the owners of these powerful
trusts misusing their influence over society
and the state. It may become especially
difficult to regulate the production of individual countries in the interest of international economic understanding, if these
countries contain powerful, independent
pyramids which stand outside of the
commonwealth.

Finally it is argued that these trusts
make it impossible for important smaller
industries to remain independent, and that
they check the initiative of the masses.

These misgivings are not entirely un-
justified. In addition, the trustification
movement has thus far failed to give one
other necessary guarantee. Trusts will, it
is true, lead to the greatest possible ration-
alization of economics, but it has not yet
been shown that these factory systems,
however technically perfect they may be,
are working towards a true collectivism.
Of what use is it to the general public, for
instance, to have the best telephone system,

if such necessities as houses, clothes, and food cannot be procured in sufficient quantities, or only at exorbitant prices? And it is also true that, up to now, every advance towards a better supply of these necessities is made retroactive through the fact that increased satisfaction constantly creates new wants. Thus, the economic pressure persists even when it is possible to satisfy all wants.

As regards the relative merits of vertical or horizontal concentration, this at least seems to be certain: Under the desperate conditions of present day German industry, the vertical trust is the most important for the near future. The merit of the horizontal system lies in its internal results. This system may be compared to a community with an economic system which allows the most suitable distribution of labor and avoids every form of industrial friction and waste of material, while at the same time enjoying unrestricted relations with the outer world. But Germany today cannot revive her industry by satisfying, however perfectly and smoothly, only her own wants. She must have free intercourse with the world. The German economic organism is crippled and will not be able to maintain itself through the coming periods of economic crises and struggles for supremacy, unless it can secure points of support and sources of food supply outside of its own borders. Only a vertical trust like that of Stinnes can create points of support for itself in the endangered districts and in foreign countries. If ten similar establishments, operating at the same stage of manufacture, join with an eleventh similar establishment in a foreign country, they cannot accomplish their economic function through the agency of this one establishment, in times of political and economic uncertainty. But a trust that is linked with the production of raw materials and is sure of disposing of its goods will be able to retain its strength in a crisis, and will even be able to engage in new forms of activity in the face of powerful obstacles.

HUGO STINNES

If we direct our attention to the anchorages of the Stinnes trust, such as Rhineland-Westphalia, Hamburg, Berlin, Bavaria, East Prussia, and German Austria, and follow out all their foreign connections, we shall find that they offer valuable guarantees of their ability to function even in periods of political and economic upheavals. If the German commonwealth succeeds in organically incorporating this powerful trust into its own economic structure, Hugo Stinnes will be one of the commonwealth's strongest pillars.